THE PORTUGUESE GUITAR CHORD BIBLE

(DABEAB Lisboa Tuning)

by

Tobe A. Richards

A Fretted Friends Publication for Cabot Books

Published by:
Cabot Books
Copyright © 2009 & 2016 by Cabot Books
All rights reserved.

First Edition September 2009
Second Edition February 2016

ISBN-13: 978-1-906207-43-4

Cabot Books
3 Kenton Mews
Henleaze
Bristol
BS9 4LT
United Kingdom

Visit our online site at www.frettedfriendsmusic.com
e-mail: cabotbooks@blueyonder.co.uk

TABLE OF CONTENTS

INTRODUCTION

The Portuguese Lisboa Guitar Chord Bible provides the musician with 1,728 chords in all keys, featuring 68 different chord types, with 3 variations of each standard chord. 144 major slash chords are also included, together with 48 moveable chord shape diagrams (providing access to a further 576 barré and standard moveable chords) making this the most comprehensive reference guide for the Portuguese Lisboa guitar currently available. For many years now, guitarists have been able to pick up a songbook and instantly play the songs in front of them, either with the help of one of the many published guides, or through the chord boxes supplied with most popular music. With the help of this *Chord Bible*, beginners and experienced Portuguese Lisboa guitar players alike will be able to take advantage of the many songbooks, fake books and musical compendiums by any artist you would care to name, from *The Beatles* to *Joan Baez*, from *Planxty* to *The Pogues* or *Springsteen* to *Simon & Garfunkel*. With 68 different chordal variations in all keys, virtually any song should be playable!

Having a good chordal knowledge should arguably be the bedrock in any fretted or keyboard musicians armoury. Whether you're playing rock, pop, folk, jazz, blues, country or other types of music, it's impossible to supply a suitable accompaniment to any vocal or solo instrumental music without providing a chordal or harmonic backing. The subtle nuance of an added ninth chord over a major chord is something that can't be captured simply by playing a melody line. In theory it is possible to approximate the harmonic intervals of any music using a limited palette of chords - probably around ten to twelve. But wherever possible it's best to use correct harmonies if they're available to you.

Having six courses of strings, the Portuguese guitar is a versatile instrument, making a wide variety of harmonic variations readily available. Despite this, sometimes compromises have to be made, particularly when a chordal configuration isn't available. But by making acceptable compromises and omitting the least important parts of that chord, even the most complex musical structures are then viable. For instance, in the case of an eleventh, the third is generally omitted without the character of the chord being adversely affected. Equally, the root or key note isn't always necessary to achieve an effective approximation of the full chord. The third is rarely missing from the majority of chords (other than elevenths) as it determines whether the key is major or minor - although this isn't a hard and fast rule, particularly in folk music where the root and fifth form the basis of most traditional music. These two intervals are generally the starting point for a number of open tunings of instruments as diverse as the guitar, the Irish bouzouki and the mountain dulcimer. The same interval is also used in a lot of heavy rock where a fifth chord is described as a *power chord*. Even though a power chord is technically neither major nor minor, it's more often used as an alternative for a major chord in most popular music.

One question which often pops up is *how many chords do I need to learn?* The smart answer is *'how long is a piece of string?'*, which is true, but it doesn't actually answer the question if you don't know where to start. My advice would be to begin with simple chord clusters like the popular G, C, D and Em progression and gradually work in new ones as you advance. If you intend playing within a rock format, it's probably sensible to learn the E, A, B sequence which is the staple of most guitarists and bassists. As a generalisation, jazz probably requires the greatest chordal knowledge of any form of music, so the learning curve will be longer if you're planning to pick up any songbook and instantly produce a recognisable version of your favourite *Duke Ellington* or *Steely Dan* number. The only truth as far as harmonic knowledge goes is you can never learn *too* much!

In this series of chord theory books, I've included a comprehensive selection of configurations of chords in all keys. As I mentioned previously, this will enable you to pick up virtually any songbook or fake book (topline melody and chord symbols) and look up the chord shape that's needed. Obviously, you'll come across the occasional song which doesn't conform to the normal harmonic intervals which you find in this, or any other chord theory publication, but with a little experimentation and experience, you'll be able to make a reasonable stab at it. For instance, most players would be more than a little bemused if they suddenly came across an instruction to play a *Gbmaj7add6/D*. Fortunately, this is fairly unusual, but from the knowledge you'll have learned, you'll be able to use a similar chord or work it out note by note. Put simply, if *every* theoretically possible chord shape were to be included in this or any other book, the result would resemble something akin to several volumes of the *Yellow Pages*!

FINGERING

Always a tricky subject and one which seems to generate a lot of discussion and differing opinions as to which method is correct. Personally, I take the view that it's a largely fruitless exercise, as the number of variables involved make a definitive answer unlikely. So what I've decided to do in this book is to choose fingering positions which feel comfortable to me. Some chord shapes will dictate the fingering used, but others will be down to personal preference. If you can practise your two and three finger chords using different fingers, it will make your playing a lot more fluid when you change to another chord shape. But if you develop habits which limit you to one playing position, it isn't the end of the world either, if you can make the transitions seamless.

The only rules, if you could loosely call them that, are:-

a) Don't abandon using your pinky or little finger if you're just beginning to play, as you'll eventually need it for some of the four finger chords which frequently crop up.

b) Try to avoid fretting with the thumb unless you're learning an instrument like the mountain dulcimer which requires a longer stretch. I know a number of players employ it on slimmer necked instruments, but I personally feel it leads to bad habits.

c) Keep your left hand fingernails short or fretting becomes a major problem. Obviously do the reverse if you're a lefty.

d) If you're a beginner and you're naturally left handed, don't get persuaded into buying a right handed instrument - it won't work! The learning curve will be steeper and you'll never get the fluidity you'd achieve with your natural hand. Most acoustic instruments can be adapted for a left hander apart from cutaway guitars and f-style mandolins etc., by reversing the nut and strings. For the non-reversible instruments, always go for a left handed model.

e) Learn to barré with other fingers apart from your index finger. This will prove invaluable with more complex chords and increase finger strength as well.

f) Don't be afraid to use fingerings further up the neck in combination with open strings as these will give you interesting new voicings and are generally quite popular in folk music. A number of these are provided in this book.

g) The Portuguese guitar is traditionally played with thumb and finger picks called *unhas*. Alternatively, standard picks or fingernails can be used if you're accustomed to this method of playing. Using a pick generally produces a much brighter sound with more attack in comparison with fingernails.

CHORD THEORY & FAQs

Q *What is a chord?*

A It's a collection of three or more notes played simultaneously. The exceptions in this book are the fourths and fifths (power chords) which aren't in the strictest sense, true chords. For convenience sake, they are classed as such.

Q *What is a triad?*

A A chord containing three notes. For example, G Major, Bm, D+ or Asus4.

Q *What are intervals?*

A Intervals are the musical distance between notes in a musical scale. For instance in the scale of C Major, C is the 1st note, D is the 2nd note, E the 3rd and so on. So if you're playing the chord of C Major, your intervals will be 1–3–5 or C as the *first* note, E as the *third* note and G as the *perfect fifth.*

Q *What is a chromatic scale and which intervals does it contain?*

A: A chromatic scale encompasses all twelve notes in a musical scale, including the sharps and flats. It's also the basis for the naming of *every* chord in existence. See the staff diagram below to see the intervals:

Q *What is a seventh chord?*

A: In its most basic form, an additional note beyond the triad. Sevenths can be either major or flattened. For instance, returning to our old friend, the key of *C*, a *Cmaj7* has an added *B* on top of the *C–E–G* triad. The resultant chord has a mellow quality often found in jazz. Now if you take the B and flatten it by dropping the fourth note in your chord down to a B flat, you get a C7.

Q: *Then why isn't it called a C minor seventh?*

A: Technically this *is* a minor seventh note, but this would create a lot of confusion when naming chords, as you already have a minor interval option in your triad (in the key of C major, E flat), so it's always referred to as a 7th to differentiate between it and a major seventh.

Q: *What is an extension?*

A: A chord which goes beyond the scope of triads and sevenths. Basically, extensions are additional notes placed above the triad or seventh in a musical stave, fingerboard or keyboard. It's important to understand these are, for theoretical purposes, always placed above the seventh. Or in layman's terms, higher up the scale. The confusion comes when you start to realise a 9th is identical to a 2nd - in the scale of C – a D note.

Q: *So why is the ninth note the same as the second note?*

A: This takes a little grasping, but if you remember that if your note goes higher than the seventh it's a 9th, but if it's lower, it'll be a 2nd. An example of this would be Csus2, which contains the root note of C, a 2nd or suspended D note and a G, the perfect 5th. You'll see this even more clearly if you look at the piano keyboard diagram below. Count from the C up to the following D beyond the 7th (B note). From the C to the second D is exactly nine whole notes.

Q: *Do any other extensions share a common note?*

A: Yes, other examples include the *11th*, which is also a *4th* and the *13th* which shares a note with the *6th*.

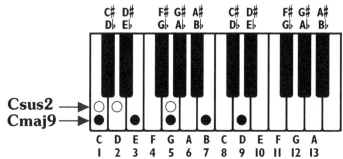

Q: *What are inversions?*

A: In the root version of a chord, the notes run in their correct order from lowest to highest. In the case of G major, it would be G–B–D. With an inversion of the same chord the notes would run in a different order. For example, the first inversion of G major would be B–D–G and the second, D–G–B. In general, triads sound more or less the same when they're inverted, but that's certainly not the case with sevenths and extensions which can sound quite different and occasionally discordant when the notes are jumbled up in certain configurations. Inversions can also produce different chords using the same basic notes. A good example of this would be *C6 (C-E-G-A)* which produces an *Am7 (A-C-E-G)* when it's inverted (both contain the notes of C–E–G–A, but in a different order). The major variations are in the tonal properties of the chords, making them sound quite different from one another.

Q: *Do elevenths and thirteenths have any particular properties?*

A: Yes. In most cases the 3rd is omitted from eleventh chords and the 11th from the majority of thirteenths as they're deemed unnecessary and arguably, create unwanted dissonance.

Q: *Some chords are called by different names in different music books. What should I do?*

A: The alternative chord name reference chart at the back of the book should help sort out the confusion.

Q: *What is a suspended chord?*

A: It's simpler to think of suspended chords as a stepping stone to a major or resolving chord. In effect the third has been left in a state of suspension by either raising it to a fourth (sus4) or lowering it to a second (sus2). Sevenths also provide versions of the suspended chord in the form of C7sus4 or C7sus2 (using the key of C as an example).

Q: *What is a diminished chord?*

A: A diminished chord has a dissonent quality to it where the third and fifth notes in a triad are flattened by a semi-tone. Again, using C as an example, C major (C-E-G) is altered to Cdim (C-E♭-G♭). A second version of a dimished chord is also used in many forms of music, the diminished seventh. This retains the elements of a standard diminished chord, adding a double flat in the seventh (C-E♭-G♭-B♭♭). A B♭♭ in this case is, to all intents and purposes, really an A note.

Q: *What is an augmented chord?*

A: An augmented chord basically performs the opposite task to a diminished one. Instead of lowering the fifth by a semitone, it raises it by the same interval. A C+ (augmented) chord contains the triad of C-E-G♯. The major root and third are retained and the fifth is sharpened.

UNDERSTANDING THE CHORD BOXES

The three diagrams below show the chord conventions illustrated in this guide. Most experienced fretted instrument players should be familiar with them. The suggested fingering positions are only meant as a general guide and will depend, in many instances, on hand size, finger length and flexibility, so feel free to experiment. The location of the black circles is unalterable, though, if you want to produce the correct voicing.

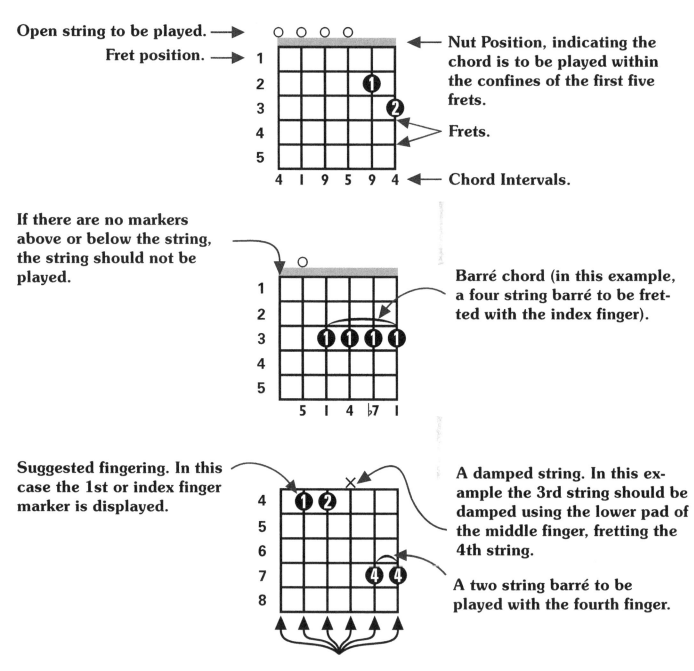

Open string to be played. →

Fret position. →

← Nut Position, indicating the chord is to be played within the confines of the first five frets.

Frets.

← Chord Intervals.

4 I 9 5 9 4

If there are no markers above or below the string, the string should not be played.

Barré chord (in this example, a four string barré to be fretted with the index finger).

5 I 4 ♭7 I

Suggested fingering. In this case the 1st or index finger marker is displayed.

A damped string. In this example the 3rd string should be damped using the lower pad of the middle finger, fretting the 4th string.

A two string barré to be played with the fourth finger.

Left to right: 6th, 5th, 4th, 3rd, 2nd and 1st courses of strings.

Whether a fretted instrument has single strings or pairs of strings, the chord boxes in this book, other chord dictionaries and songbooks treat it as a four stringed instrument. This convention is common to all double or triple course instruments such as the mandolin or tiple, making the diagrams a lot less confusing and free from unnecessary clutter.

PORTUGUESE LISBOA GUITAR FINGERBOARD & TUNING LAYOUT

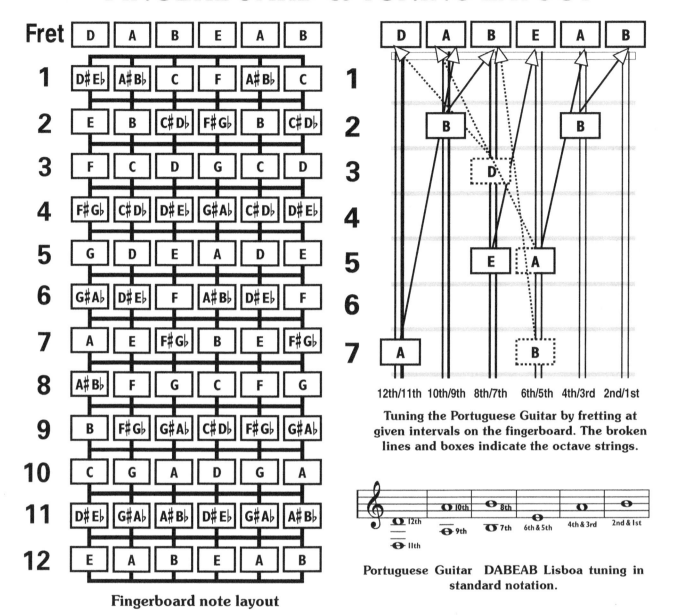

Fingerboard note layout

Tuning the Portuguese Guitar by fretting at given intervals on the fingerboard. The broken lines and boxes indicate the octave strings.

Portuguese Guitar DABEAB Lisboa tuning in standard notation.

To tune your Portuguese Lisboa guitar accurately, it's best to use an electronic chromatic tuner, but if there isn't one available, you can tune it to a guitar or piano/electronic keyboard. The following tuning grid gives the correct fingering positions on the guitar fingerboard and piano keyboard.

Portuguese Lisboa Guitar	Guitar	Piano
1st & 2nd string (B)	1st string (E) fretted at the 7th fret	1st B above middle C
3rd & 4th string (A)	1st string (E) fretted at the 5th fret	1st A above middle C
5th & 6th string (E)	1st open string (E)	1st E below middle C
7th string (B)	2nd open string (B)	1st B below middle C
8th octave string (B)	1st string (E) fretted at 7th fret	1st B above middle C
9th string (A)	3rd string (G) fretted at 2nd fret	1st A below middle C
10th octave string (A)	1st string (E) fretted at 5th fret	1st A below middle C
11th string (D)	4th open string (D)	1st D below middle C
12th octave string (D)	2nd string (B) fretted at 3rd fret	1st D above middle C

THE CHORDS COVERED IN THIS BOOK

Chord	Chord Name in Full	Harmonic Interval
C	Major	1–3–5
Cm	Minor	1–F3-5
C-5	Major Diminished Fifth	1–3–F5
C°	Diminished	1–F3--F5
C4	Fourth	1–4
C5	Fifth or Power Chord	1–5
Csus2	Suspended Second	1–2–5
Csus4	Suspended Fourth	1–4–5
Csus4add9	Suspended Fourth Added Ninth	1–4–5–9
C+	Augmented	1–3–S5
C6	Major Sixth	1–3–5–6
Cadd9	Major Added Ninth	1–3–5–9
Cadd11	Major Added Eleventh	1–3–5–11
Cm6	Minor Sixth	1–F3–5–6
Cm-6	Minor Diminished Sixth	1–F3–5–F6
Cmadd9	Minor Added Ninth	1–F3–5–9
C6add9	Major Sixth Added Ninth	1–3–5–6–9
Cm6add9	Minor Sixth Added Ninth	1–F3–5–6–9
C°7	Diminished Seventh	1–F3–F5–DF7
C7	Seventh	1–3–5–F7
C7sus2	Seventh Suspended Second	1–2–5–F7
C7sus4	Seventh Suspended Fourth	1–4–5–F7
C7-5	Seventh Diminished Fifth	1–3–F5–F7
C7+5	Seventh Augmented Fifth	1–3–S5–F7
C7-9	Seventh Minor Ninth	1–3–5–F7–F9
C7+9	Seventh Augmented Ninth	1–3–5–F7–S9
C7-5-9	Seventh Diminished Fifth Minor Ninth	1–3–F5–F7–F9
C7-5+9	Seventh Diminished Fifth Augmented Ninth	1–3–F5–F7–S9
C7+5-9	Seventh Augmented Fifth Minor Ninth	1–3–S5–F7–F9
C7+5+9	Seventh Augmented Fifth Augmented Ninth	1–3–S5–F7–S9
C7add11	Seventh Added Eleventh	1–3–5–F7–11
C7+11	Seventh Augmented Eleventh	1–3–5–F7–S11
C7add13	Seventh Added Thirteenth	1–3–5–F7–13
Cm7	Minor Seventh	1–F3–5–F7
Cm7-5	Minor Seventh Diminished Fifth	1–F3–F5–F7
Cm7-5-9	Minor Seventh Diminished Fifth Minor Ninth	1–F3–F5–F7–F9
Cm7-9	Minor Seventh Minor Ninth	1–F3–5–F7–F9
Cm7add11	Minor Seventh Added Eleventh	1–F3–5–F7–11
Cm(maj7)	Minor Major Seventh	1–F3–5–7
Cmaj7	Major Seventh	1–3–5–7
Cmaj7-5	Major Seventh Diminished Fifth	1–3–F5–7
Cmaj7+5	Major Seventh Augmented Fifth	1–3–S5–7
Cmaj7+11	Major Seventh Augmented Eleventh	1–3–5–7–S11
C9	Ninth	1–3–5–F7–9
C9sus4	Ninth Suspended Fourth	1–4–5–F7–9
C9-5	Ninth Diminished Fifth	1–3–F5–F7–9
C9+5	Ninth Augmented Fifth	1–3–S5–F7–9
C9+11	Ninth Augmented Eleventh	1–3–5–F7–9–S11
Cm9	Minor Ninth	1–F3–5–F7–9

Chord	Chord Name in Full	Harmonic Interval
Cm9-5	Minor Ninth Diminished Fifth	1–F3–F5–F7–9
Cm(maj9)	Minor Major Ninth	1–F3–5–7–9
Cmaj9	Major Ninth	1–3–5–7–9
Cmaj9-5	Major Ninth Diminished Fifth	1–3–F5–7–9
Cmaj9+5	Major Ninth Augmented Fifth	1–3–S5–7–9
Cmaj9add6	Major Ninth Added Sixth	1–3–5–6–7–9
Cmaj9+11	Major Ninth Augmented Eleventh	1–3–5–7–9–S11
C11	Eleventh	1–3–5–F7–9–11
C11-9	Eleventh Diminished Ninth	1–3–5–F7–F9–11
Cm11	Minor Eleventh	1–F3–5–F7–9–11
Cmaj11	Major Eleventh	1–3–5–7–9–11
C13	Thirteenth	1–3–5–F7–9–11–13
C13sus4	Thirteenth Suspended Fourth	1–4–5–F7–9–11–13
C13-5-9	Thirteenth Diminished Fifth Minor Ninth	1–3–F5–F7–F9–11–13
C13-9	Thirteenth Minor Ninth	1–3–5–F7–F9–11–13
C13+9	Thirteenth Augmented Ninth	1–3–5–F7–S9–11–13
C13+11	Thirteenth Augmented Eleventh	1–3–5–F7–9–S11–13
Cm13	Minor Thirteenth	1–F3–5–F7–9–11–13
Cmaj13	Major Thirteenth	1–3–5–7–9–11–13

Key: F = Flat   S = Sharp   DF = Double Flat

SLASH CHORDS

What is a slash chord? Put simply, they're standard chords with an added note in the bass. *So what differentiates a C chord from a C/G when the G is already part of that chord, in this case, the fifth?* Theoretically, nothing, but the difference is very apparent when you actually sound the chord. The G bass is emphasised to provide a different feel to the harmonics. Slashes are also commonly found when the music calls for a descending bassline. For example; C, C/B, C/A and C/G.

The note after the slash indicates the bass note being played. For instance A/E would be an instruction to play a A chord with a E bass.

Slash Note. Generally found on the 6th & 5th or 4th courses.

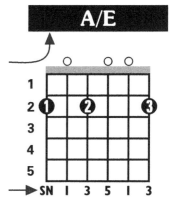

How do I play a slash chord that isn't listed in this book? Well, firstly, it would be an almost impossible task to cover every possible slash chord in existence, because the variations are potentially even greater than with standard chords. What you can do, within the confines of this guide, is to find the part of the chord before the slash in the main body of the book and then look for the nearest bass note on the fifth or sixth course of strings. To find the right bass note, consult the fingerboard layout on *page 9*.

USING A CAPO (OR *CAPO D'ASTRA*)

Using a capo is a quick and easy way of changing key to suit a different vocal range or to join in with with other musicians playing in a different key. For the uniniated, a capo is a moveable bar that clamps onto the fingerboard of fretted instruments. It works in much the same way as using a finger barré to hold down the strings. They come in a variety of designs and prices, the simplest using a metal rod covered in rubber and sprung with elastic. For the Portuguese Guitar, look for a guitar capo suitable for a curved fingerboard.

C Chords

C
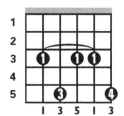

Cm
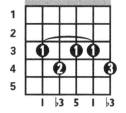

C7
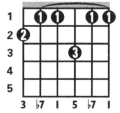

Cm7
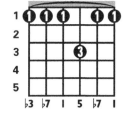

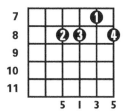
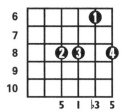
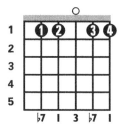
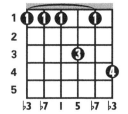

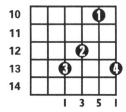
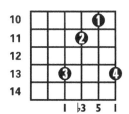
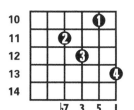
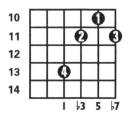

C5
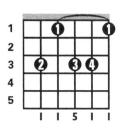

C6
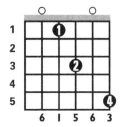

Cm6
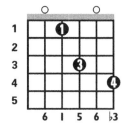

Cmaj7
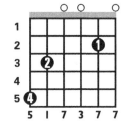

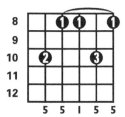
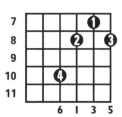
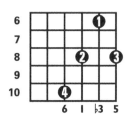
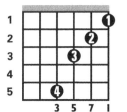

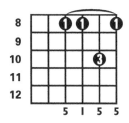
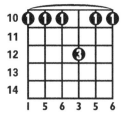
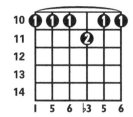
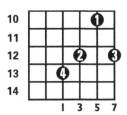

C Chords

C°
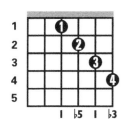
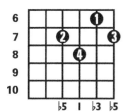
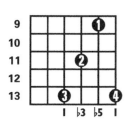

C°7
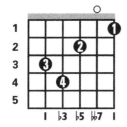
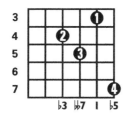
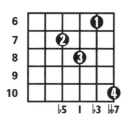

C-5
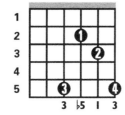
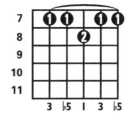
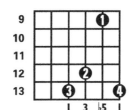

C+
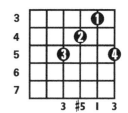
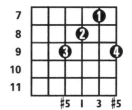
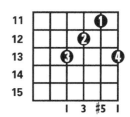

Csus2
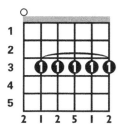
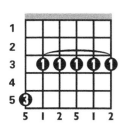
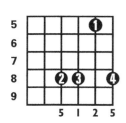

Csus4
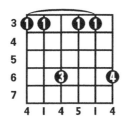
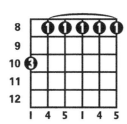
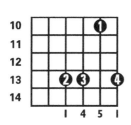

C7sus4
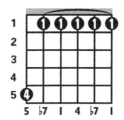
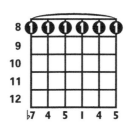
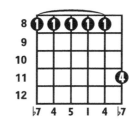

Cm7-5

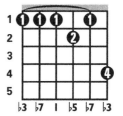
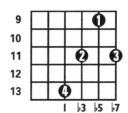

C Chords

Cadd9
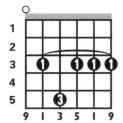
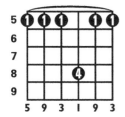
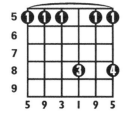

Cmadd9
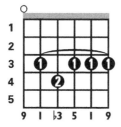
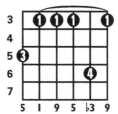
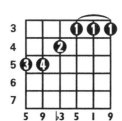

C6add9
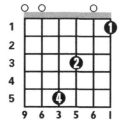
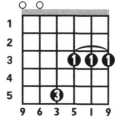
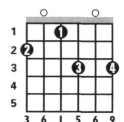

Cm6add9
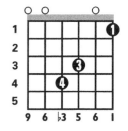
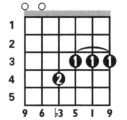
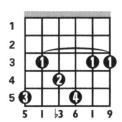

C7-5
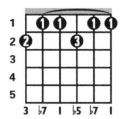
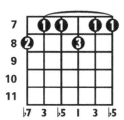
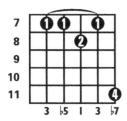

C7+5
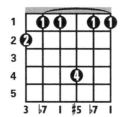
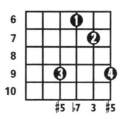
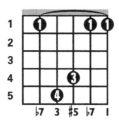

C7-9
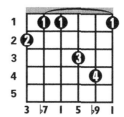
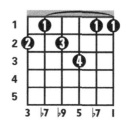
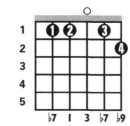

C7+9
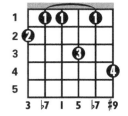
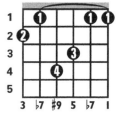
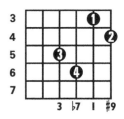

14

C Chords

Cm(maj7)
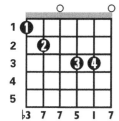
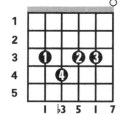
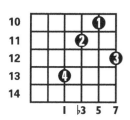

Cmaj7-5
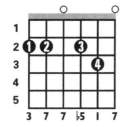
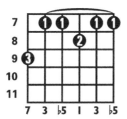
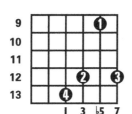

Cmaj7+5
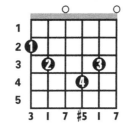
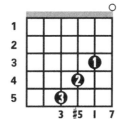
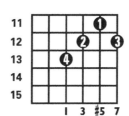

C9
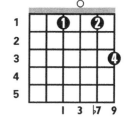
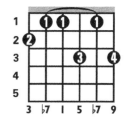
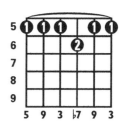

Cm9
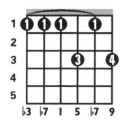
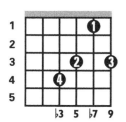
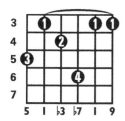

Cmaj9
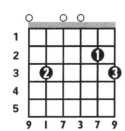
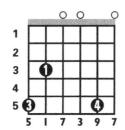
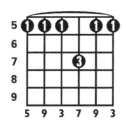

C11
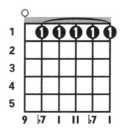
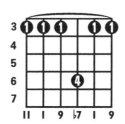
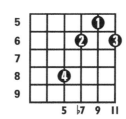

C13
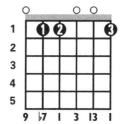
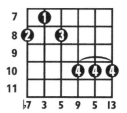
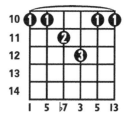

15

C Chords (Advanced)

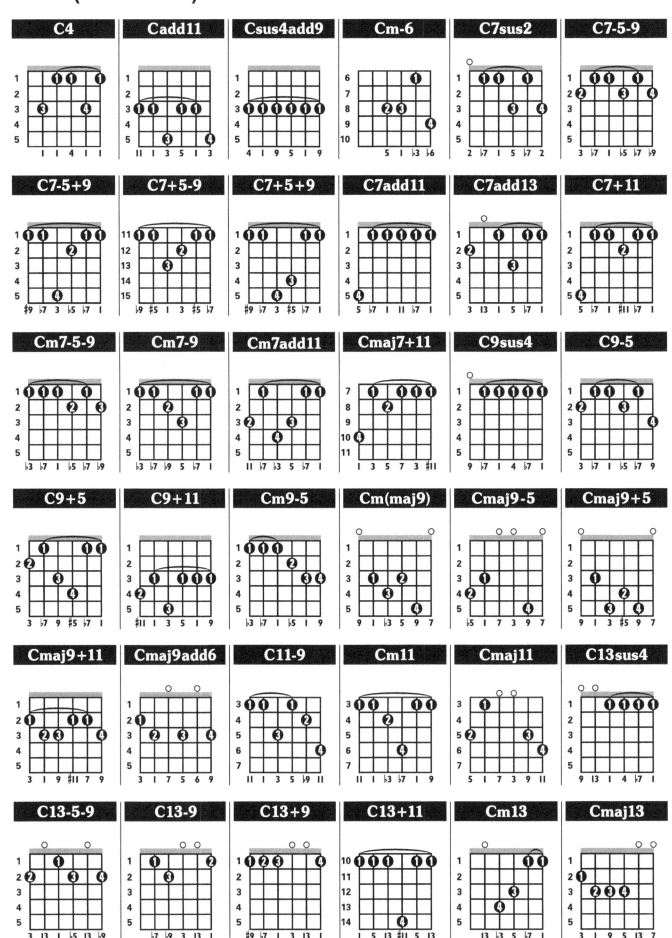

Db

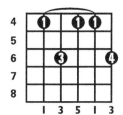

Dbm

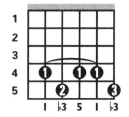

Db7

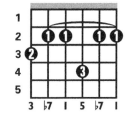

Dbm7

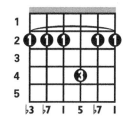

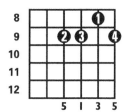

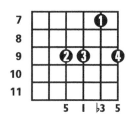

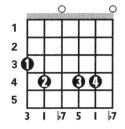

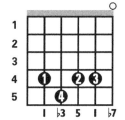

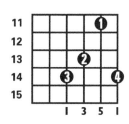

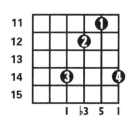

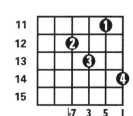

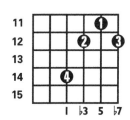

Db5

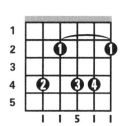

Db6

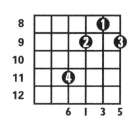

Dbm6

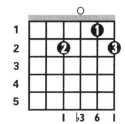

Dbmaj7

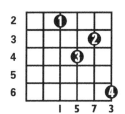

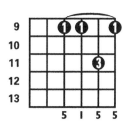

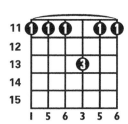

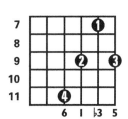

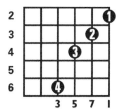

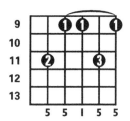

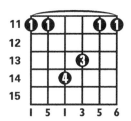

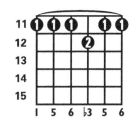

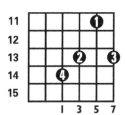

17

C# / D♭ Chords

D♭°
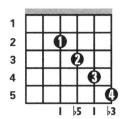
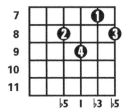
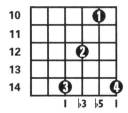

D♭°7
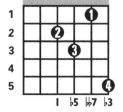
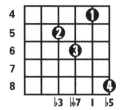
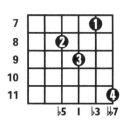

D♭-5
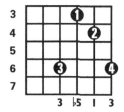
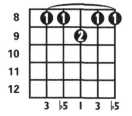
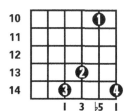

D♭+
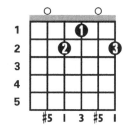
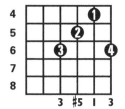
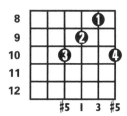

D♭sus2
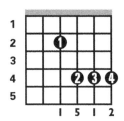
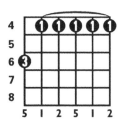
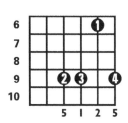

D♭sus4
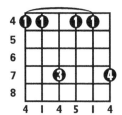
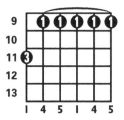
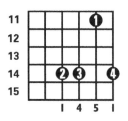

D♭7sus4
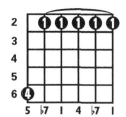
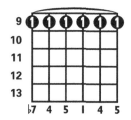
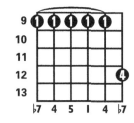

D♭m7-5
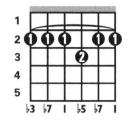
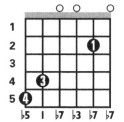
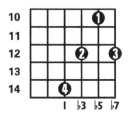

Dbadd9
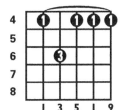
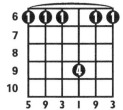
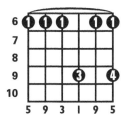

Dbmadd9
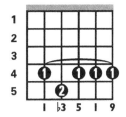
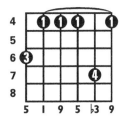
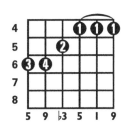

Db6add9

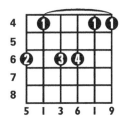
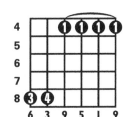

Dbm6add9
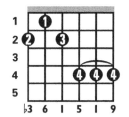
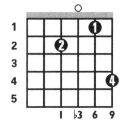
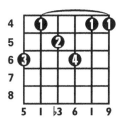

Db7-5
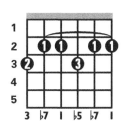
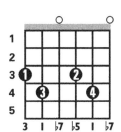
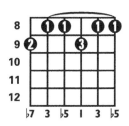

Db7+5
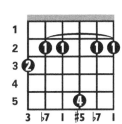
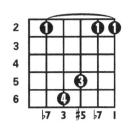
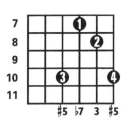

Db7-9
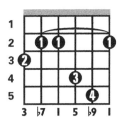
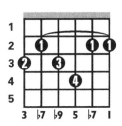
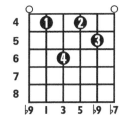

Db7+9
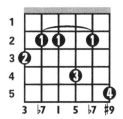
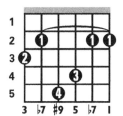
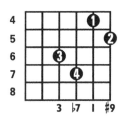

19

C♯/ D♭ Chords

D♭m(maj7)
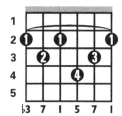
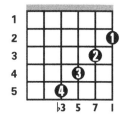
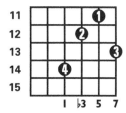

D♭maj7-5
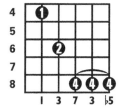
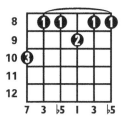
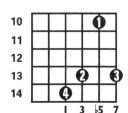

D♭maj7+5
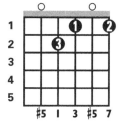
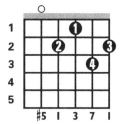
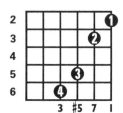

D♭9
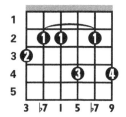
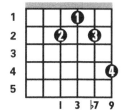

D♭m9
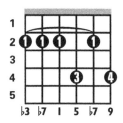
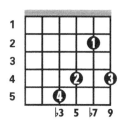
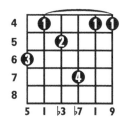

D♭maj9
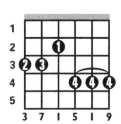
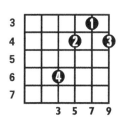
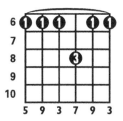

D♭11
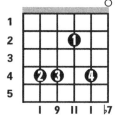
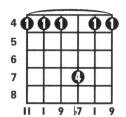
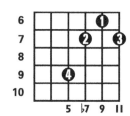

D♭13
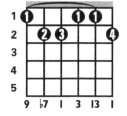
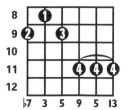
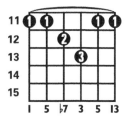

20

C#/ D♭ Chords (Advanced)

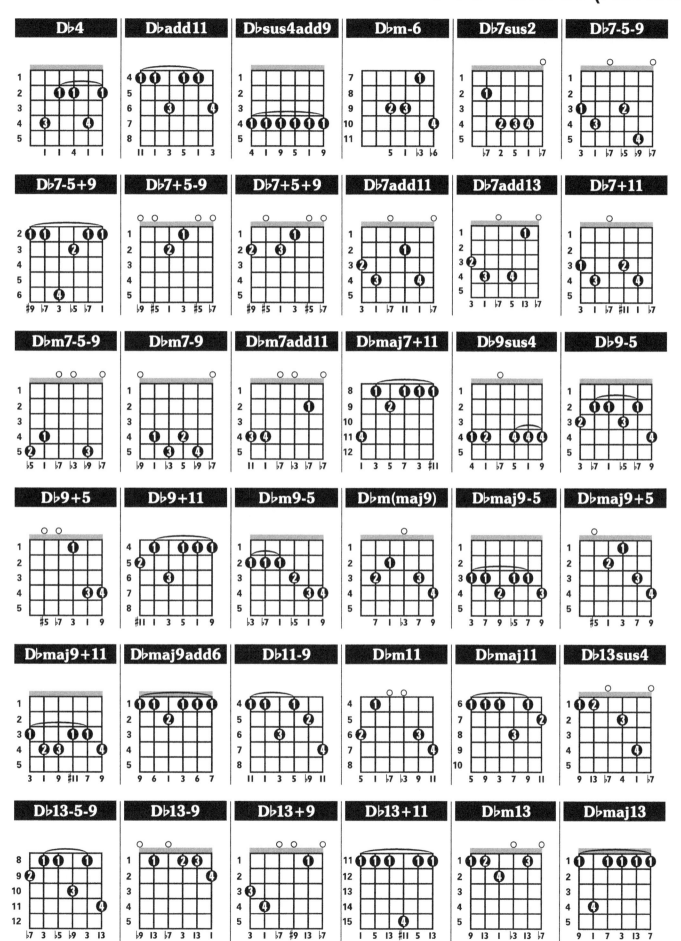

21

D Chords

D

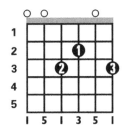

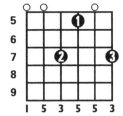

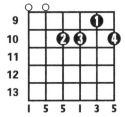

Dm

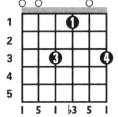

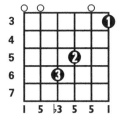

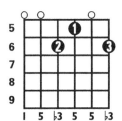

D7

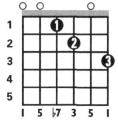

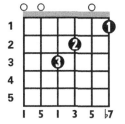

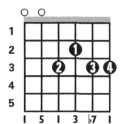

Dm7

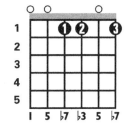

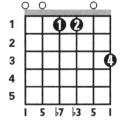

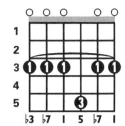

D5

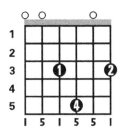

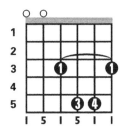

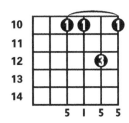

D6

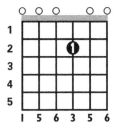

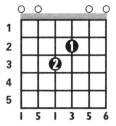

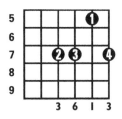

Dm6

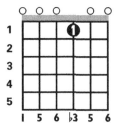

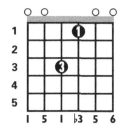

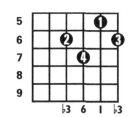

Dmaj7

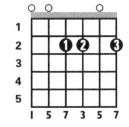

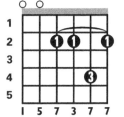

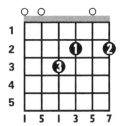

D Chords

D°

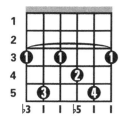

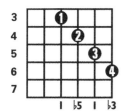

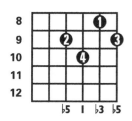

D°7

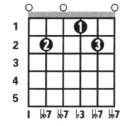

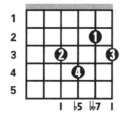

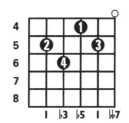

D-5

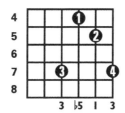

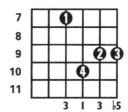

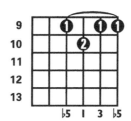

D+

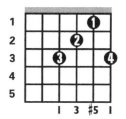

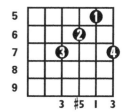

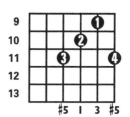

Dsus2

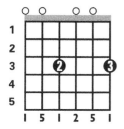

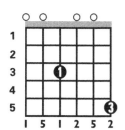

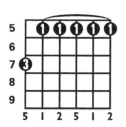

Dsus4

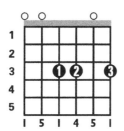

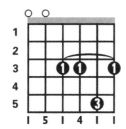

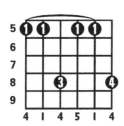

D7sus4

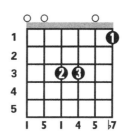

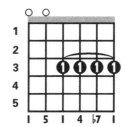

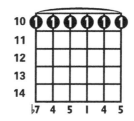

Dm7-5

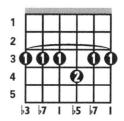

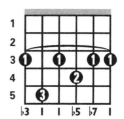

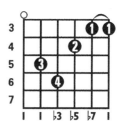

23

D Chords

Dadd9
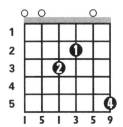
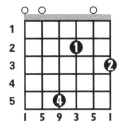
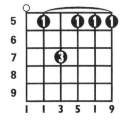

Dmadd9
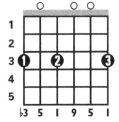
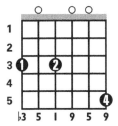
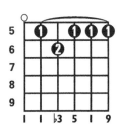

D6add9
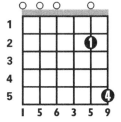
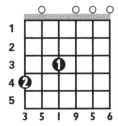
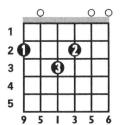

Dm6add9
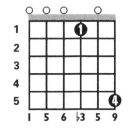
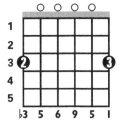
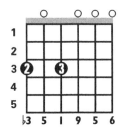

D7-5
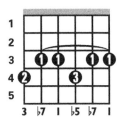
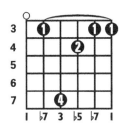
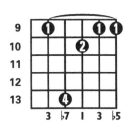

D7+5
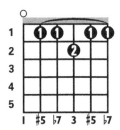
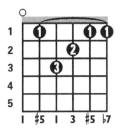
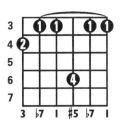

D7-9
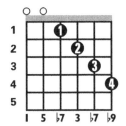
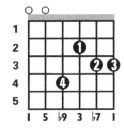
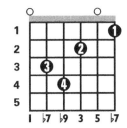

D7+9
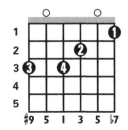
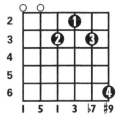
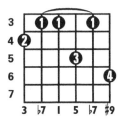

D Chords

Dm(maj7)
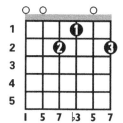
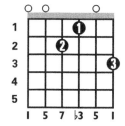
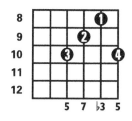

Dmaj7-5
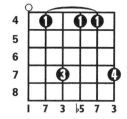
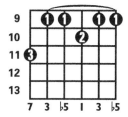
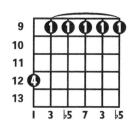

Dmaj7+5
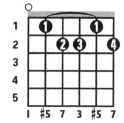
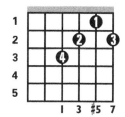
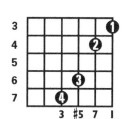

D9
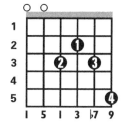
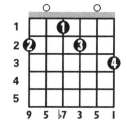
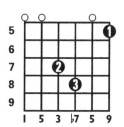

Dm9
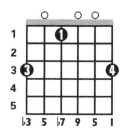
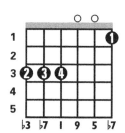
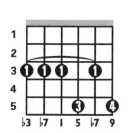

Dmaj9
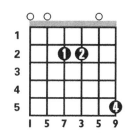
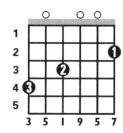
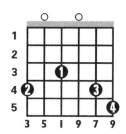

D11
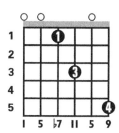
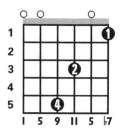
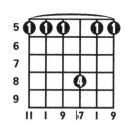

D13
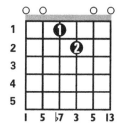
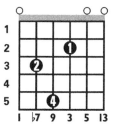
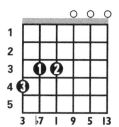

25

D Chords (Advanced)

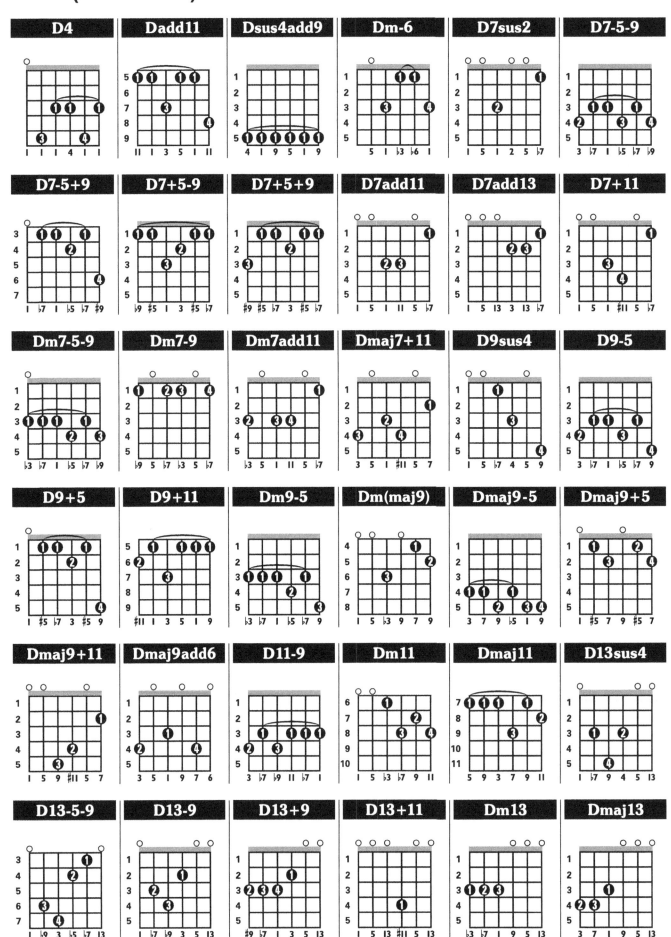

E♭
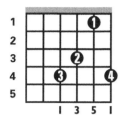
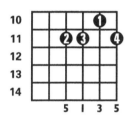
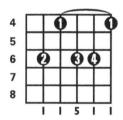

E♭m
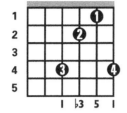
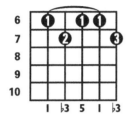
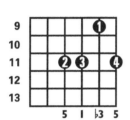

E♭7
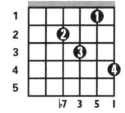
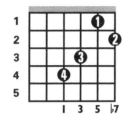
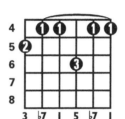

E♭m7
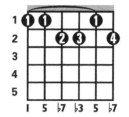
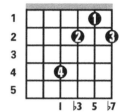
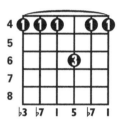

E♭5
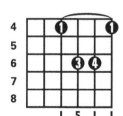
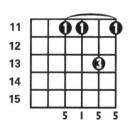

E♭6

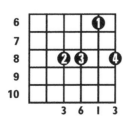

E♭m6
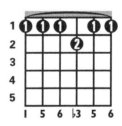
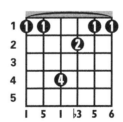
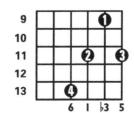

E♭maj7
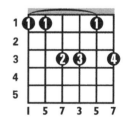
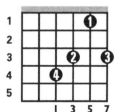
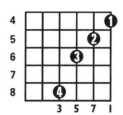

27

D#/ Eb Chords

Ebo

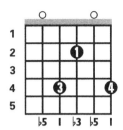

Ebo7

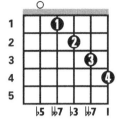

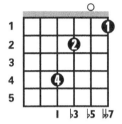

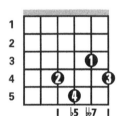

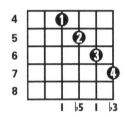

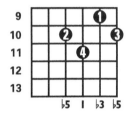

Eb-5

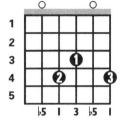

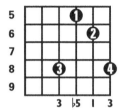

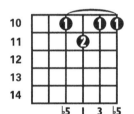

Eb+

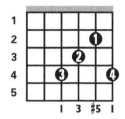

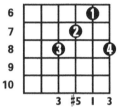

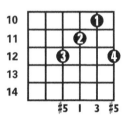

Ebsus2

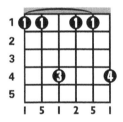

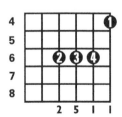

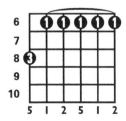

Ebsus4

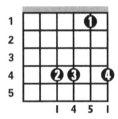

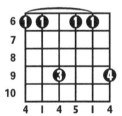

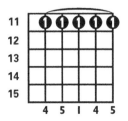

Eb7sus4

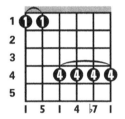

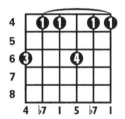

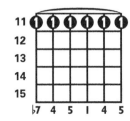

Ebm7-5

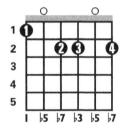

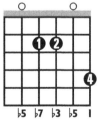

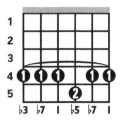

28

E♭add9
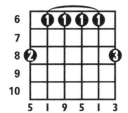
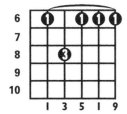
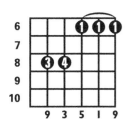

E♭madd9
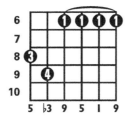
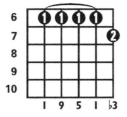
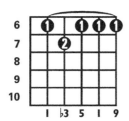

E♭6add9
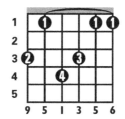
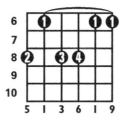
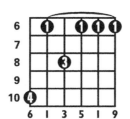

E♭m6add9
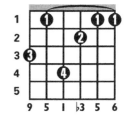
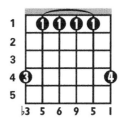
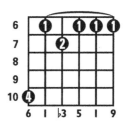

E♭7-5
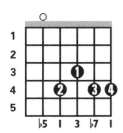
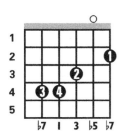
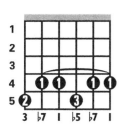

E♭7+5
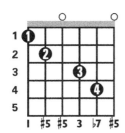
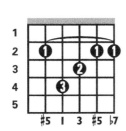
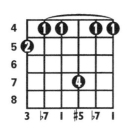

E♭7-9
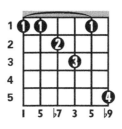
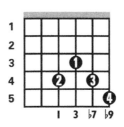
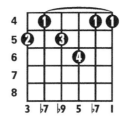

E♭7+9
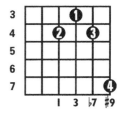
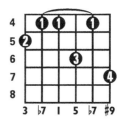
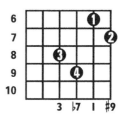

D#/ E♭ Chords

E♭m(maj7)

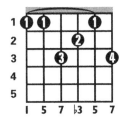

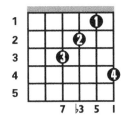

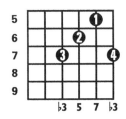

E♭maj7-5

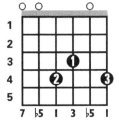

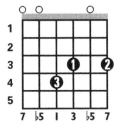

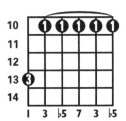

E♭maj7+5

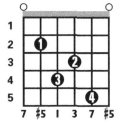

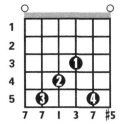

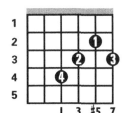

E♭9

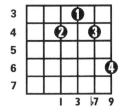

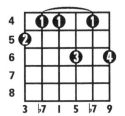

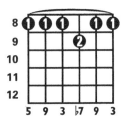

E♭m9

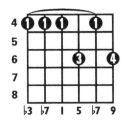

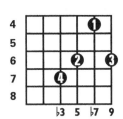

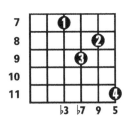

E♭maj9

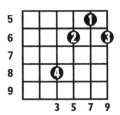

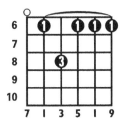

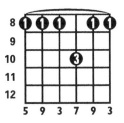

E♭11

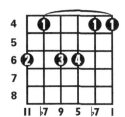

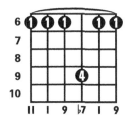

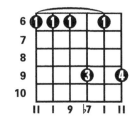

E♭13

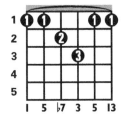

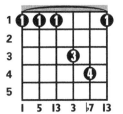

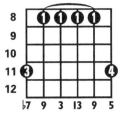

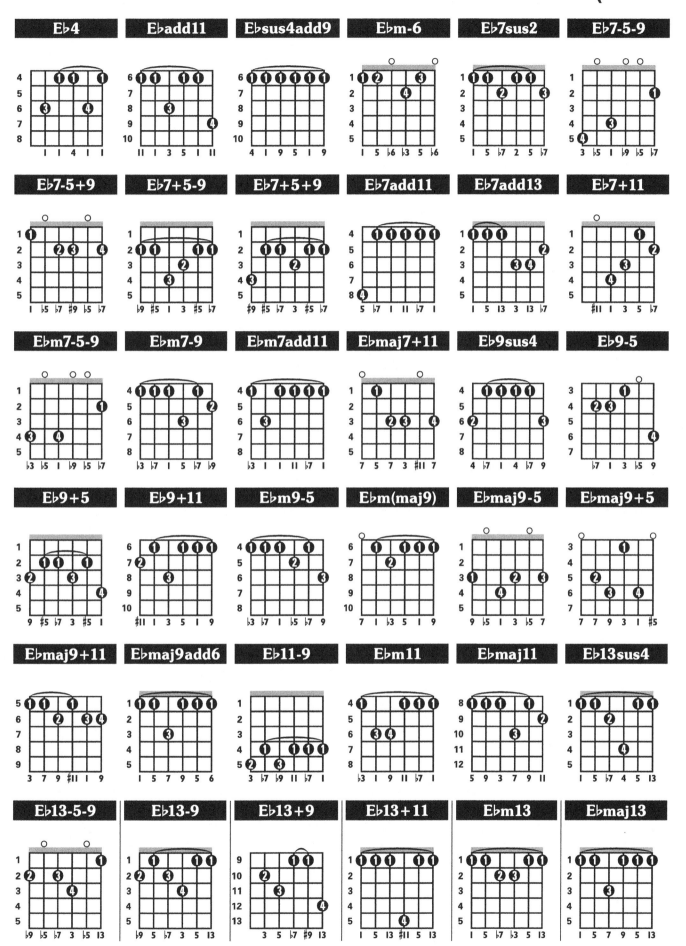

E Chords

E	Em	E7	Em7
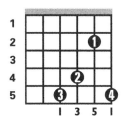	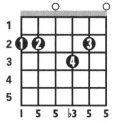	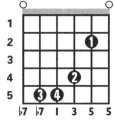	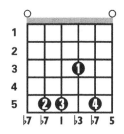
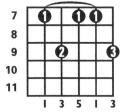	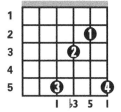	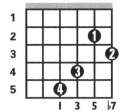	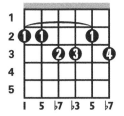
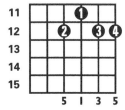	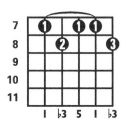	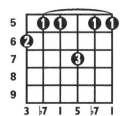	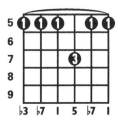

E5	E6	Em6	Emaj7
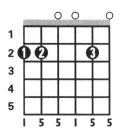	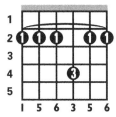	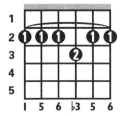	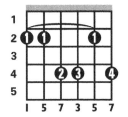
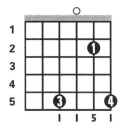	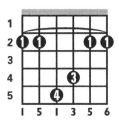	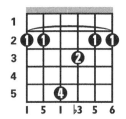	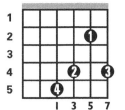
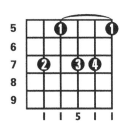	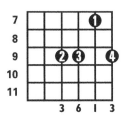	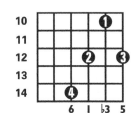	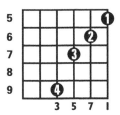

E Chords

E°	E°7	E-5	E+

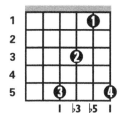 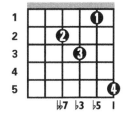 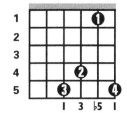 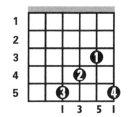

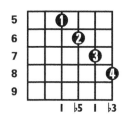 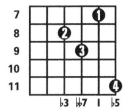 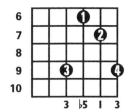 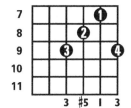

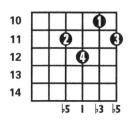 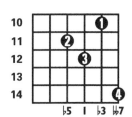 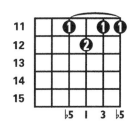 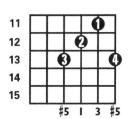

Esus2	Esus4	E7sus4	Em7-5

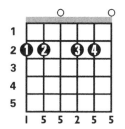 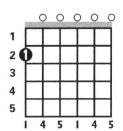 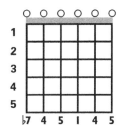 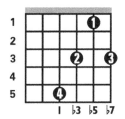

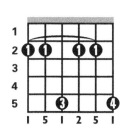 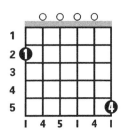 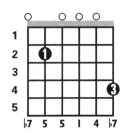 

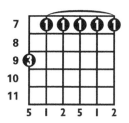 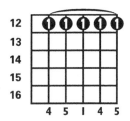 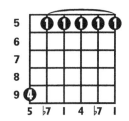 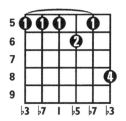

33

E Chords

Eadd9	Emadd9	E6add9	Em6add9
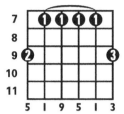	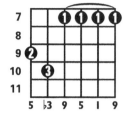	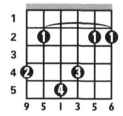	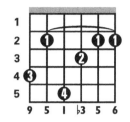
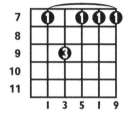	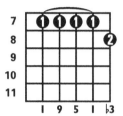	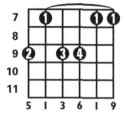	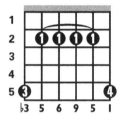
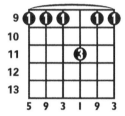	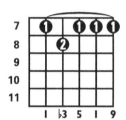	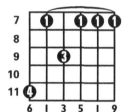	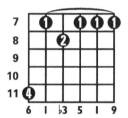

E7-5	E7+5	E7-9	E7+9
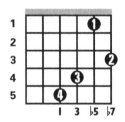	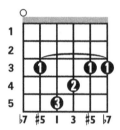	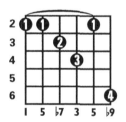	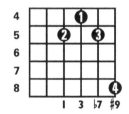
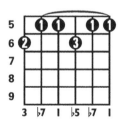	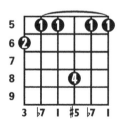	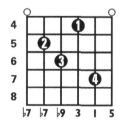	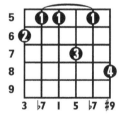
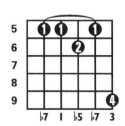	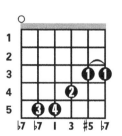	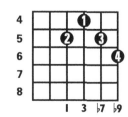	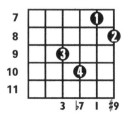

Em(maj7)

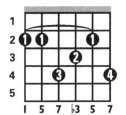

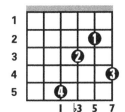

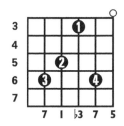

Emaj7-5

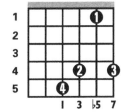

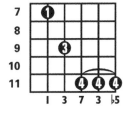

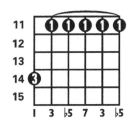

Emaj7+5

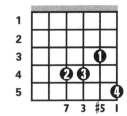

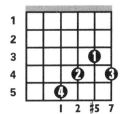

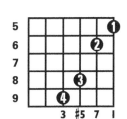

E9

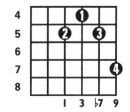

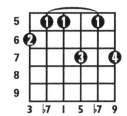

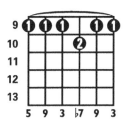

Em9

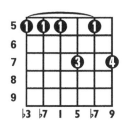

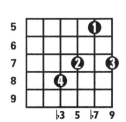

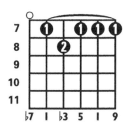

Emaj9

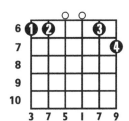

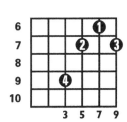

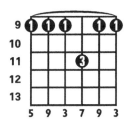

E11

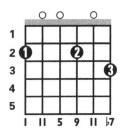

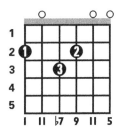

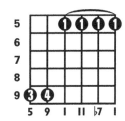

E13

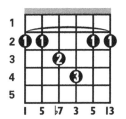

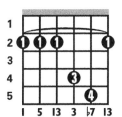

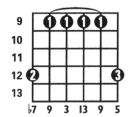

E Chords (Advanced)

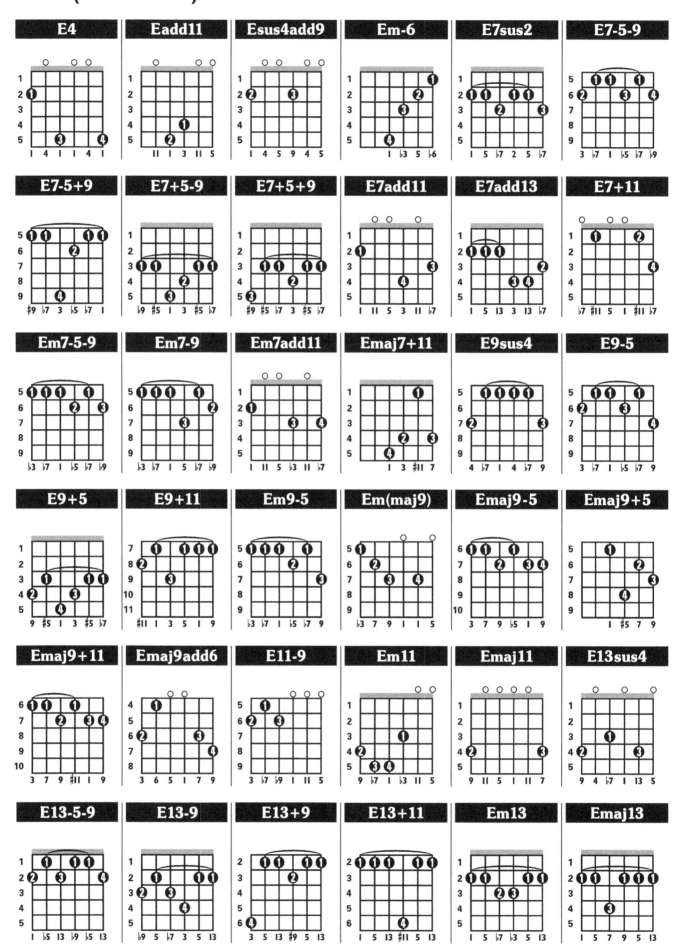

F Chords

F

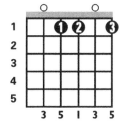

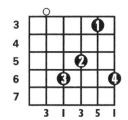

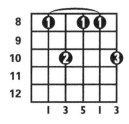

Fm

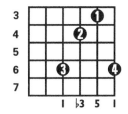

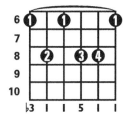

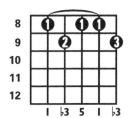

F7

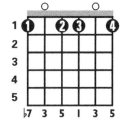

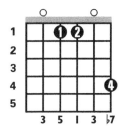

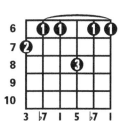

Fm7

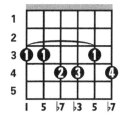

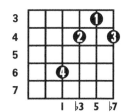

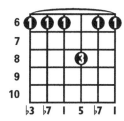

F5

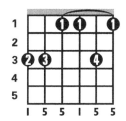

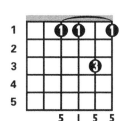

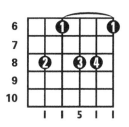

F6

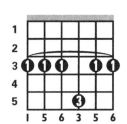

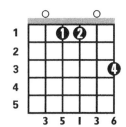

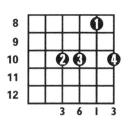

Fm6

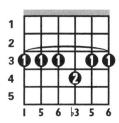

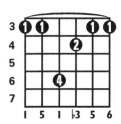

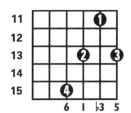

Fmaj7

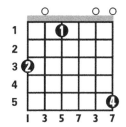

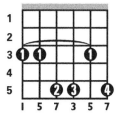

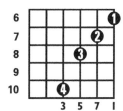

37

F Chords

Fº

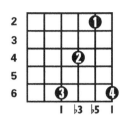

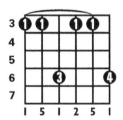

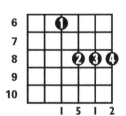

Fº7

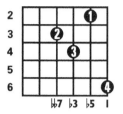

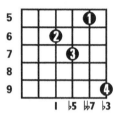

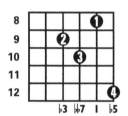

F-5

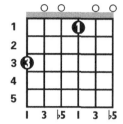

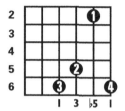

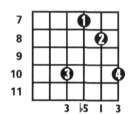

F+

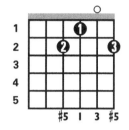

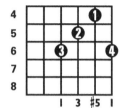

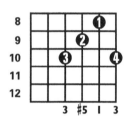

Fsus2

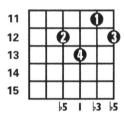

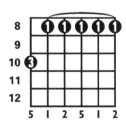

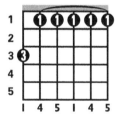

Fsus4

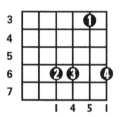

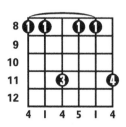

F7sus4

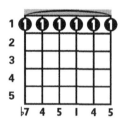

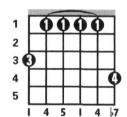

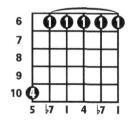

Fm7-5

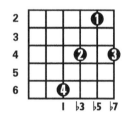

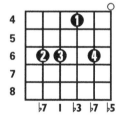

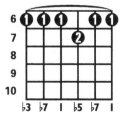

38

F Chords

Fadd9
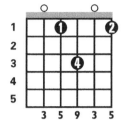

3 5 9 3 5

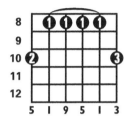

5 1 9 5 1 3

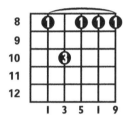

1 3 5 1 9

Fmadd9
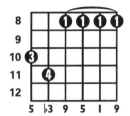

5 b3 9 5 1 9

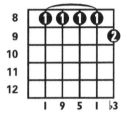

1 9 5 1 b3

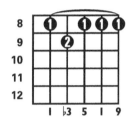

1 b3 5 1 9

F6add9
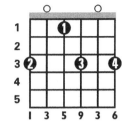

1 3 5 9 3 6

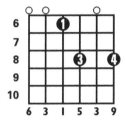

6 3 1 5 3 9

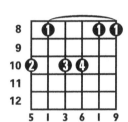

5 1 3 6 1 9

Fm6add9
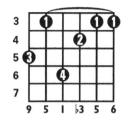

9 5 1 b3 5 6

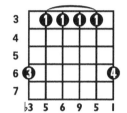

b3 5 6 9 5 1

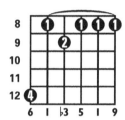

6 1 b3 5 1 9

F7-5
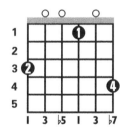

1 3 b5 1 3 b7

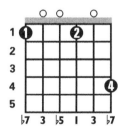

b7 3 b5 1 3 b7

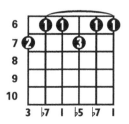

3 b7 1 b5 b7 1

F7+5
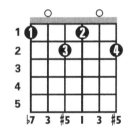

b7 3 #5 1 3 #5

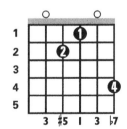

3 #5 1 3 b7

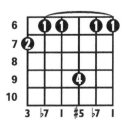

3 b7 1 #5 b7 1

F7-9
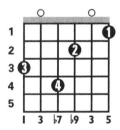

1 3 b7 b9 3 5

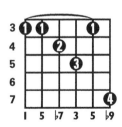

1 5 b7 3 5 b9

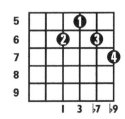

1 3 b7 b9

F7+9
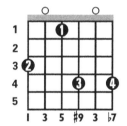

1 3 5 #9 3 b7

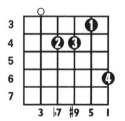

3 b7 #9 5 1

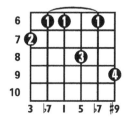

3 b7 1 5 b7 #9

39

F Chords

Fadd9

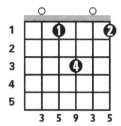

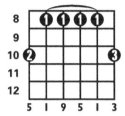

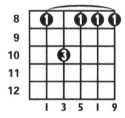

Fmadd9

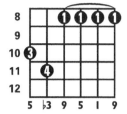

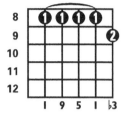

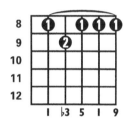

F6add9

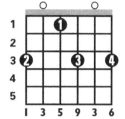

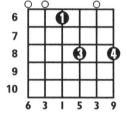

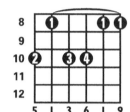

Fm6add9

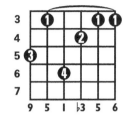

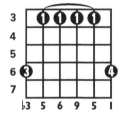

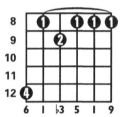

F7-5

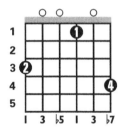

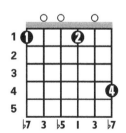

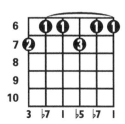

F7+5

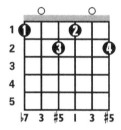

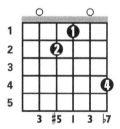

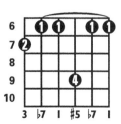

F7-9

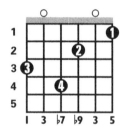

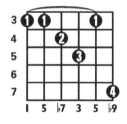

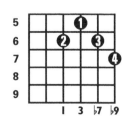

F7+9

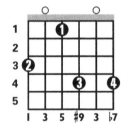

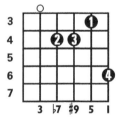

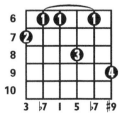

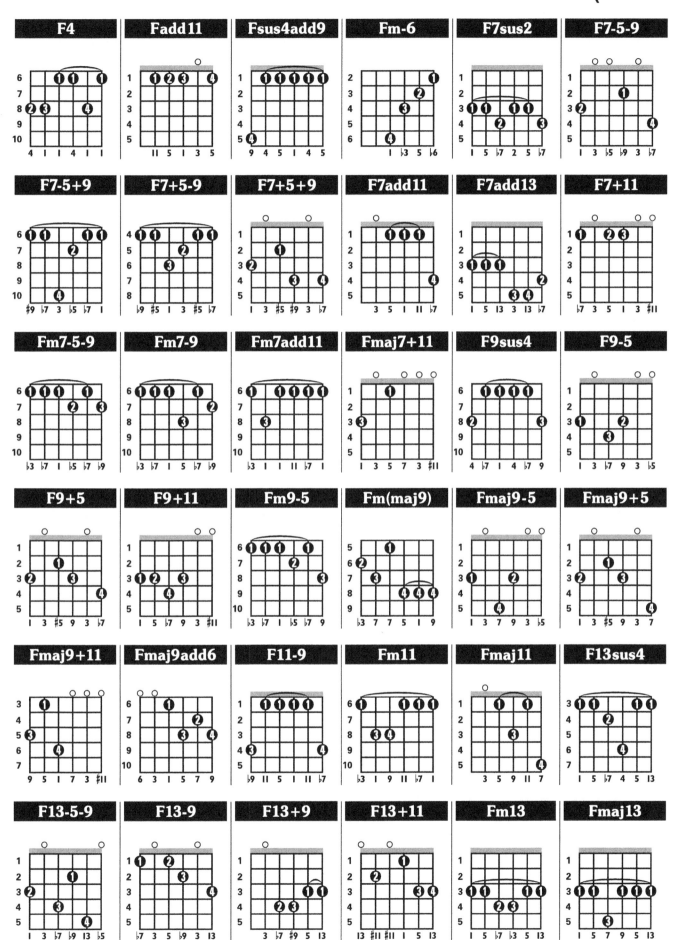

F# / G♭ Chords

F#	F#m	F#7	F#m7

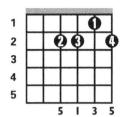
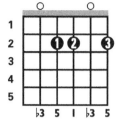
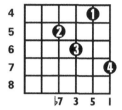
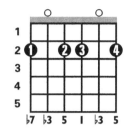

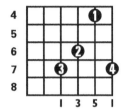
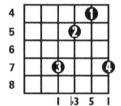
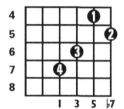
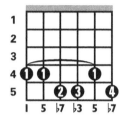

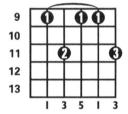
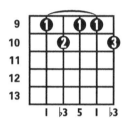
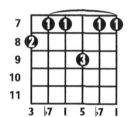
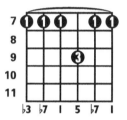

F#5	F#6	F#m6	F#maj7

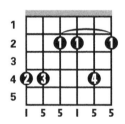
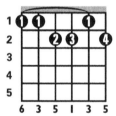
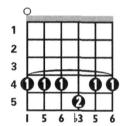
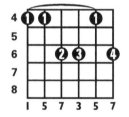

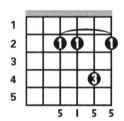
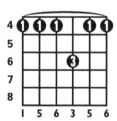
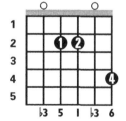
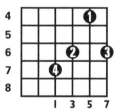

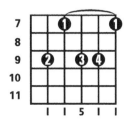
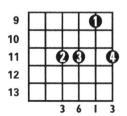
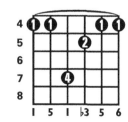
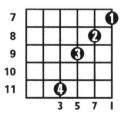

F#°
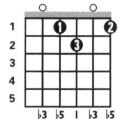
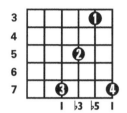
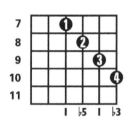

F#°7
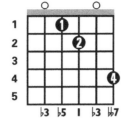
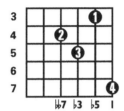
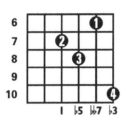

F#-5
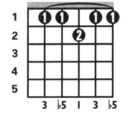
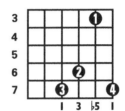
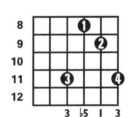

F#+
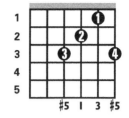
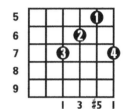
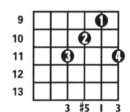

F#sus2
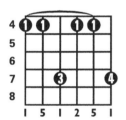
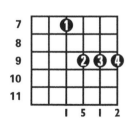
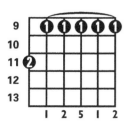

F#sus4
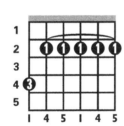
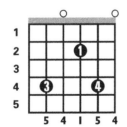
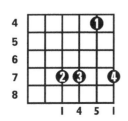

F#7sus4
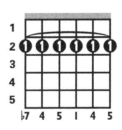
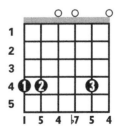
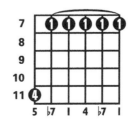

F#m7-5
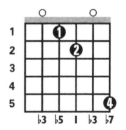
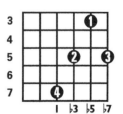
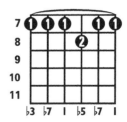

F#/ G♭ Chords

F#add9

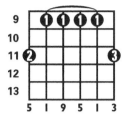

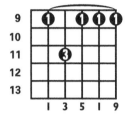

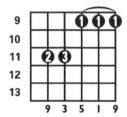

F#madd9

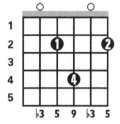

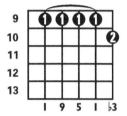

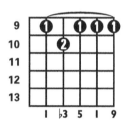

F#6add9

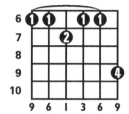

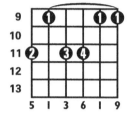

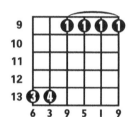

F#m6add9

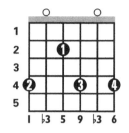

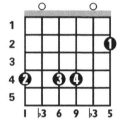

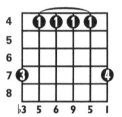

F#7-5

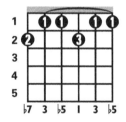

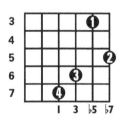

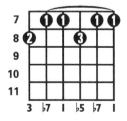

F#7+5

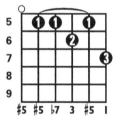

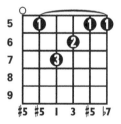

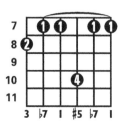

F#7-9

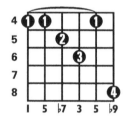

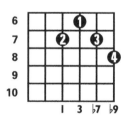

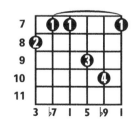

F#7+9

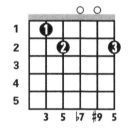

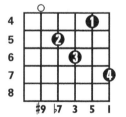

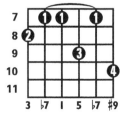

F#/ Gb Chords

F#m(maj7)
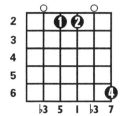
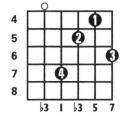
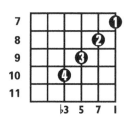

F#maj7-5
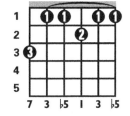
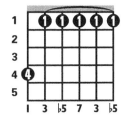
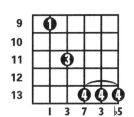

F#maj7+5
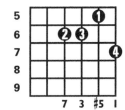
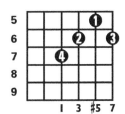
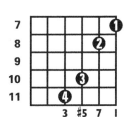

F#9
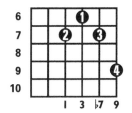
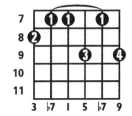
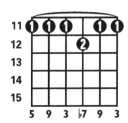

F#m9
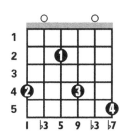
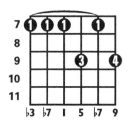
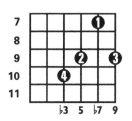

F#maj9
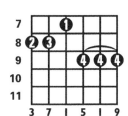
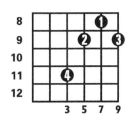
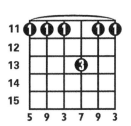

F#11
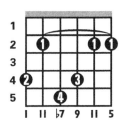
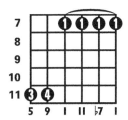
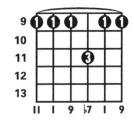

F#13
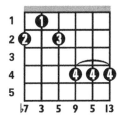
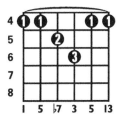
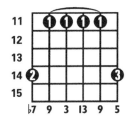

45

F#/ G♭ Chords (Advanced)

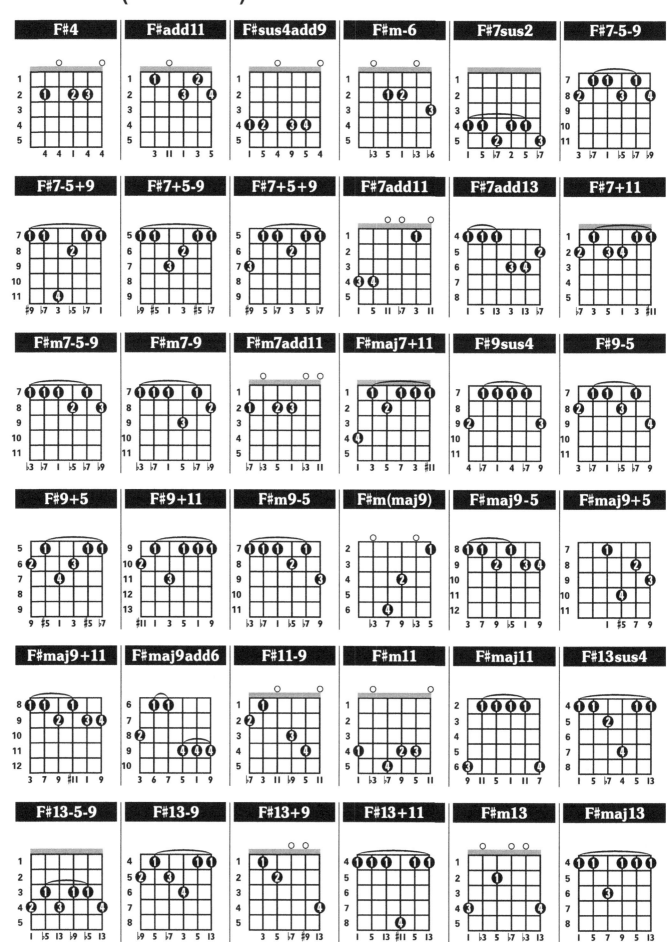

G Chords

G

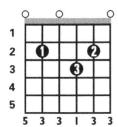
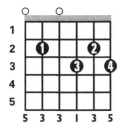
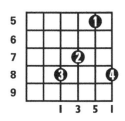

Gm

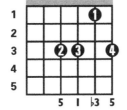
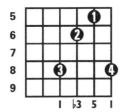
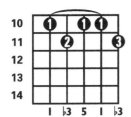

G7

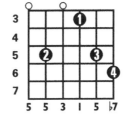
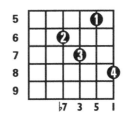
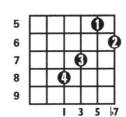

Gm7

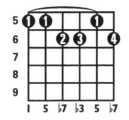
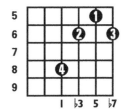
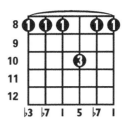

G5

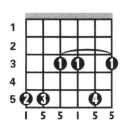
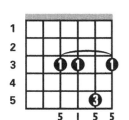
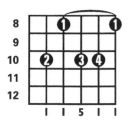

G6

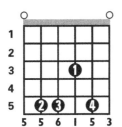

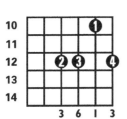

Gm6

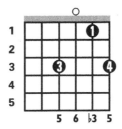
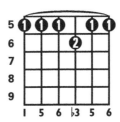
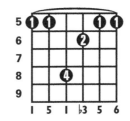

Gmaj7

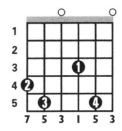
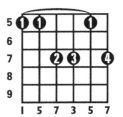
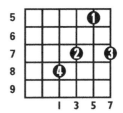

47

G Chords

G°	G°7	G-5	G+

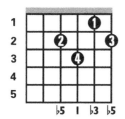 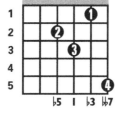 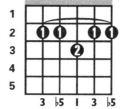 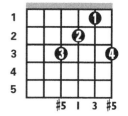

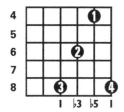 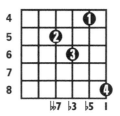 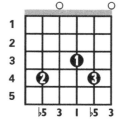 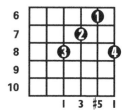

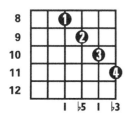 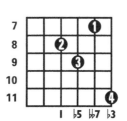 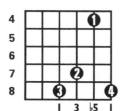 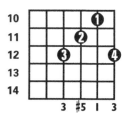

Gsus2	Gsus4	G7sus4	Gm7-5

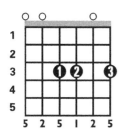 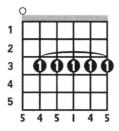 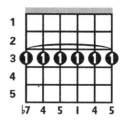 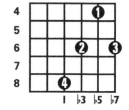

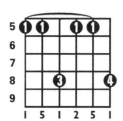 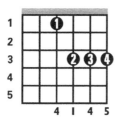 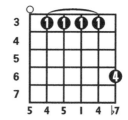 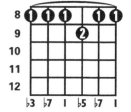

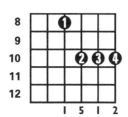 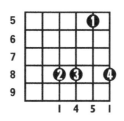 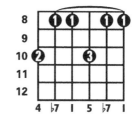 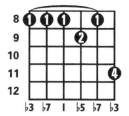

G Chords

Gadd9

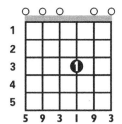

5 9 3 1 9 3

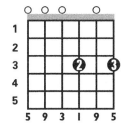

5 9 3 1 9 5

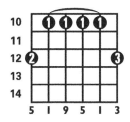

5 1 9 5 1 3

Gmadd9

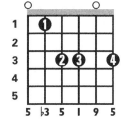

5 b3 5 1 9 5

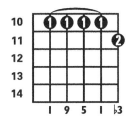

1 9 5 1 b3

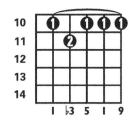

1 b3 5 1 9

G6add9

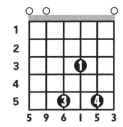

5 9 6 1 5 3

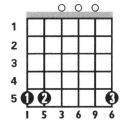

1 5 3 6 9 6

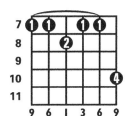

9 6 1 3 6 9

Gm6add9

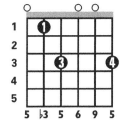

5 b3 5 6 9 5

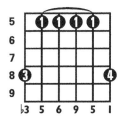

b3 5 6 9 5 1

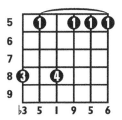

b3 5 1 9 5 6

G7-5

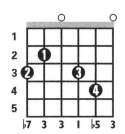

b7 3 3 1 b5 3

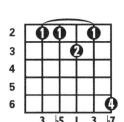

3 b5 1 3 b7

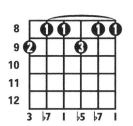

3 b7 1 b5 b7 1

G7+5

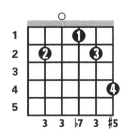

3 3 b7 3 #5

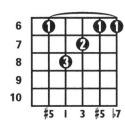

#5 1 3 #5 b7

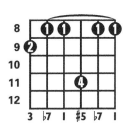

3 b7 1 #5 b7 1

G7-9

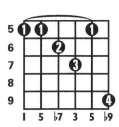

1 5 b7 3 5 b9

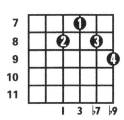

1 3 b7 b9

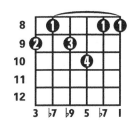

3 b7 b9 5 b7 1

G7+9

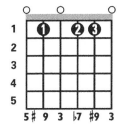

5 # 9 3 b7 #9 3

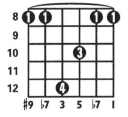

#9 b7 3 5 b7 1

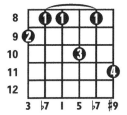

3 b7 1 5 b7 #9

49

G Chords

Gm(maj7)

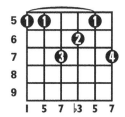
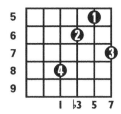
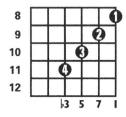

Gmaj7-5

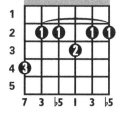
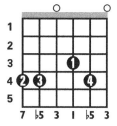
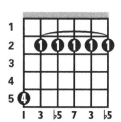

Gmaj7+5

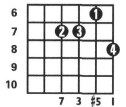
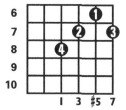
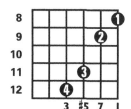

G9

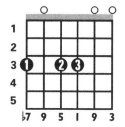
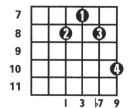
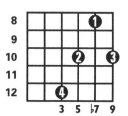

Gm9

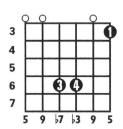
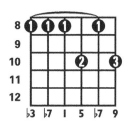
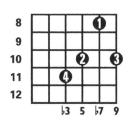

Gmaj9

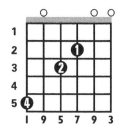
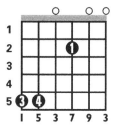
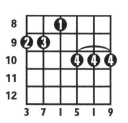

G11

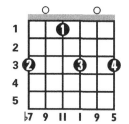
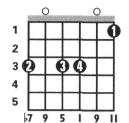
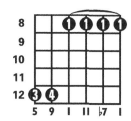

G13

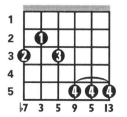
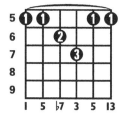

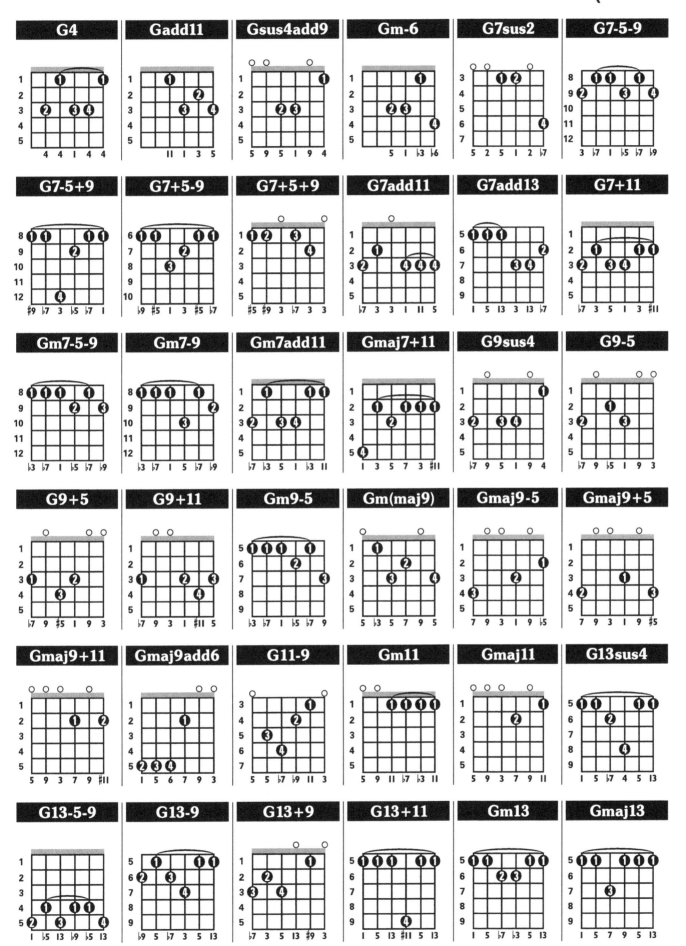

G# / A♭ Chords

A♭
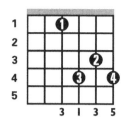
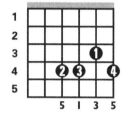
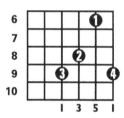

A♭m
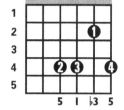
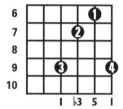
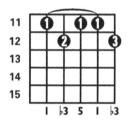

A♭7
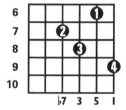
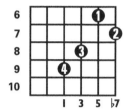
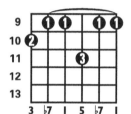

A♭m7
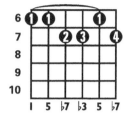
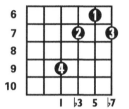
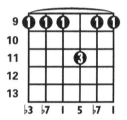

A♭5
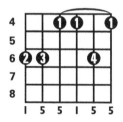
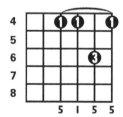
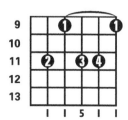

A♭6
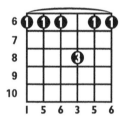
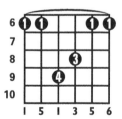
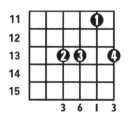

A♭m6
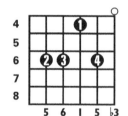
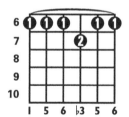
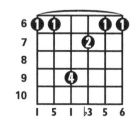

A♭maj7
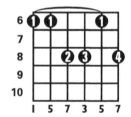
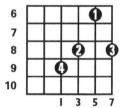
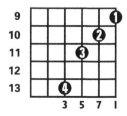

A♭°
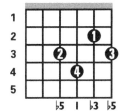
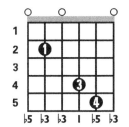
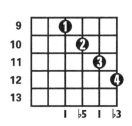

A♭°7
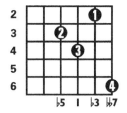
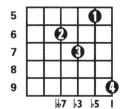
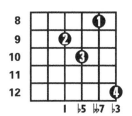

A♭-5
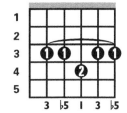
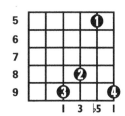
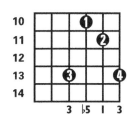

A♭+
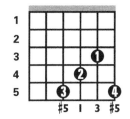
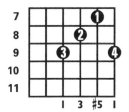
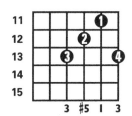

A♭sus2
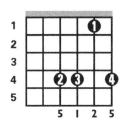
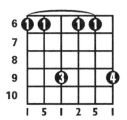
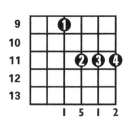

A♭sus4
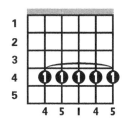
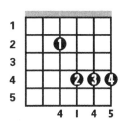
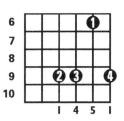

A♭7sus4
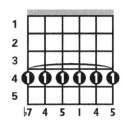
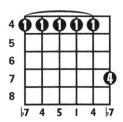
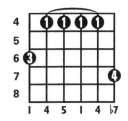

A♭m7-5
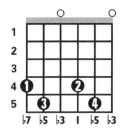
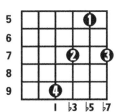
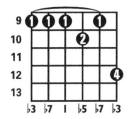

G# / A♭ Chords

A♭add9

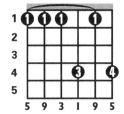
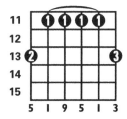

A♭madd9
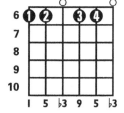
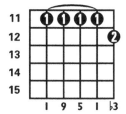
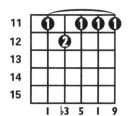

A♭6add9
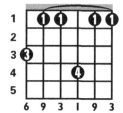
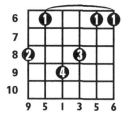
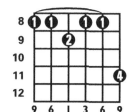

A♭m6add9
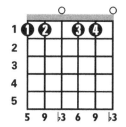
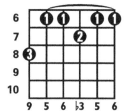
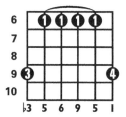

A♭7-5
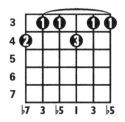
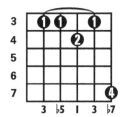
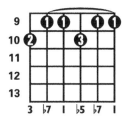

A♭7+5
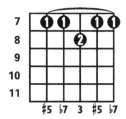
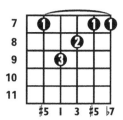
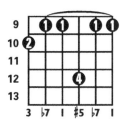

A♭7-9
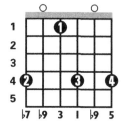
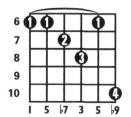
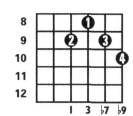

A♭7+9
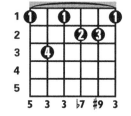
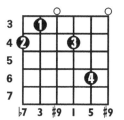
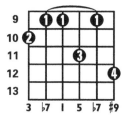

A♭m(maj7)
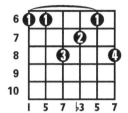
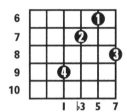
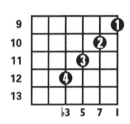

A♭maj7-5
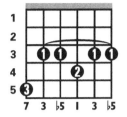
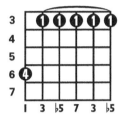
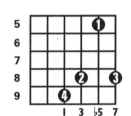

A♭maj7+5
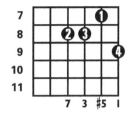
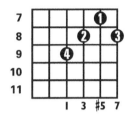
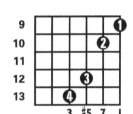

A♭9
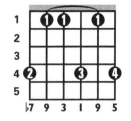
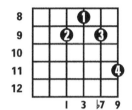
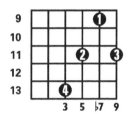

A♭m9
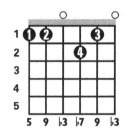
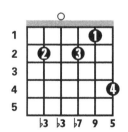
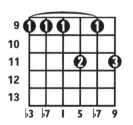

A♭maj9

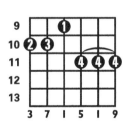
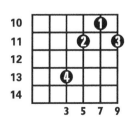

A♭11
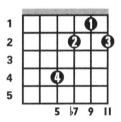

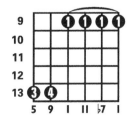

A♭13
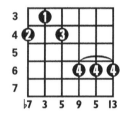
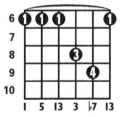
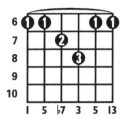

G# / A♭ Chords (Advanced)

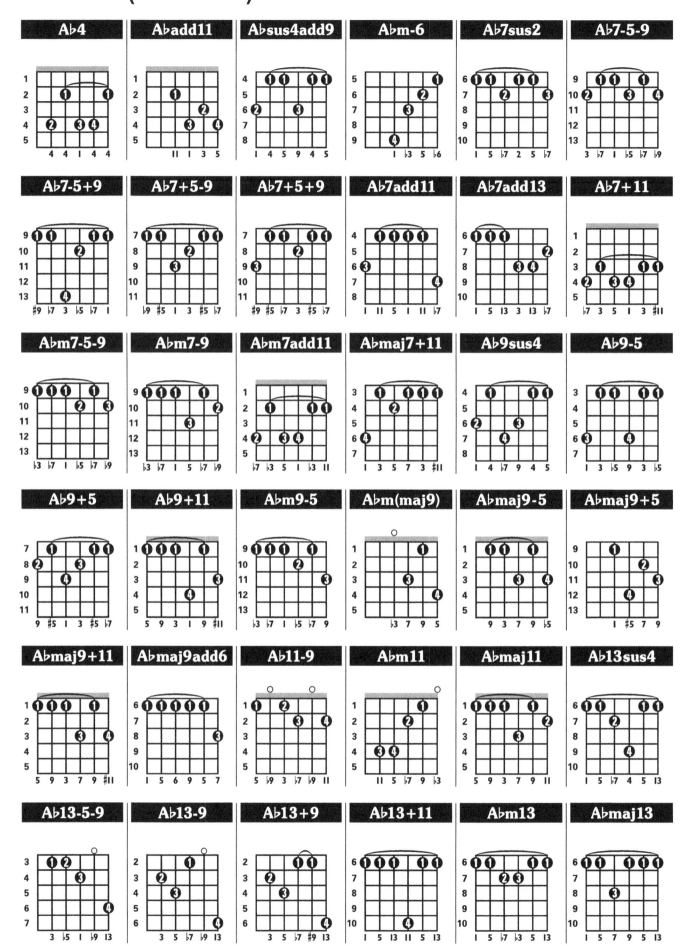

A Chords

A

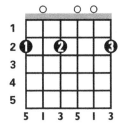

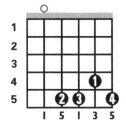

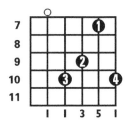

Am

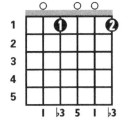

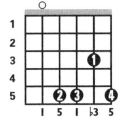

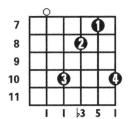

A7

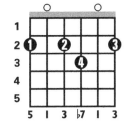

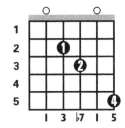

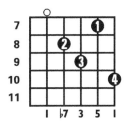

Am7

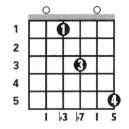

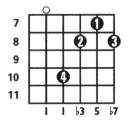

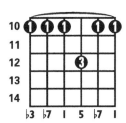

A5

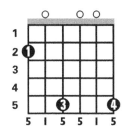

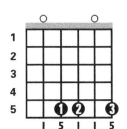

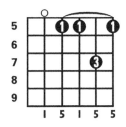

A6

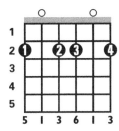

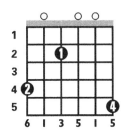

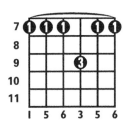

Am6

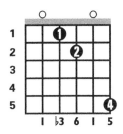

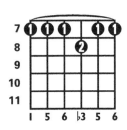

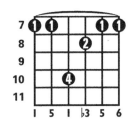

Amaj7

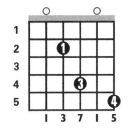

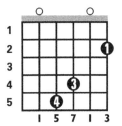

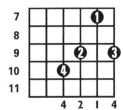

A Chords

A°
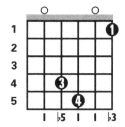
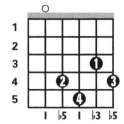
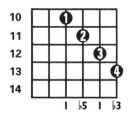

A°7
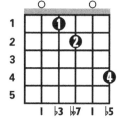
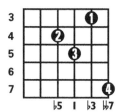
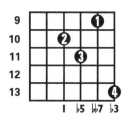

A-5
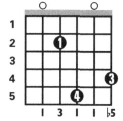
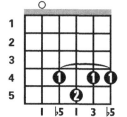
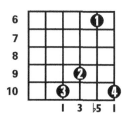

A+
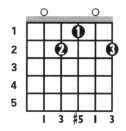
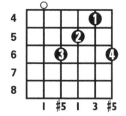
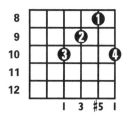

Asus2
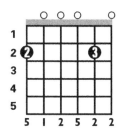
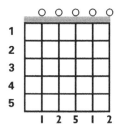
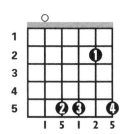

Asus4
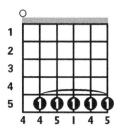
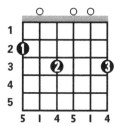
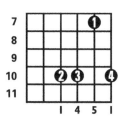

A7sus4
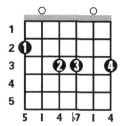
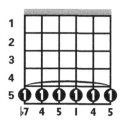
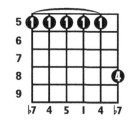

Am7-5
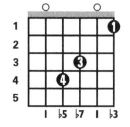
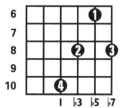
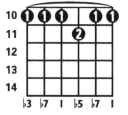

A Chords

Aadd9

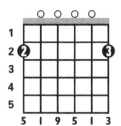

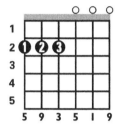

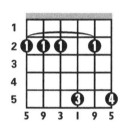

Amadd9

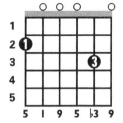

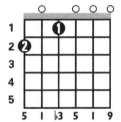

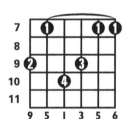

A6add9

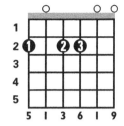

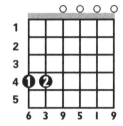

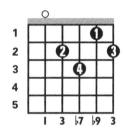

Am6add9

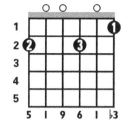

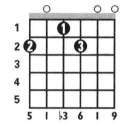

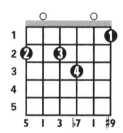

A7-5

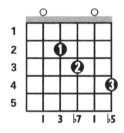

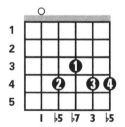

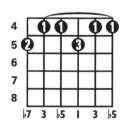

A7+5

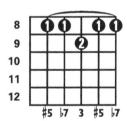

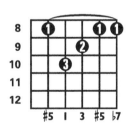

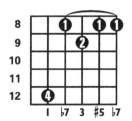

A7-9

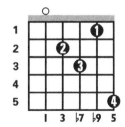

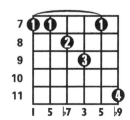

A7+9

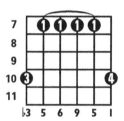

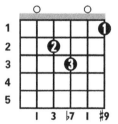

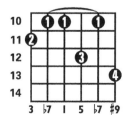

59

A Chords

Am(maj7)
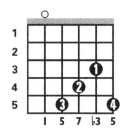
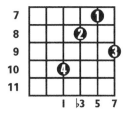
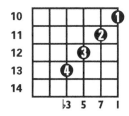

Amaj7-5
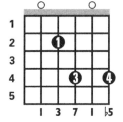
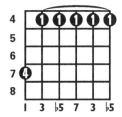
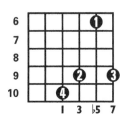

Amaj7+5
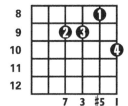
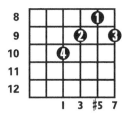
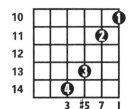

A9
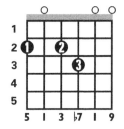
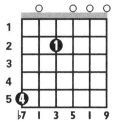
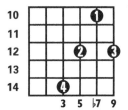

Am9
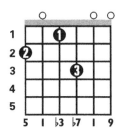
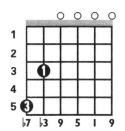
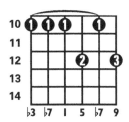

Amaj9
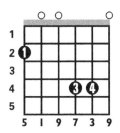
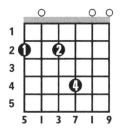
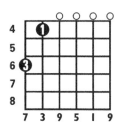

A11
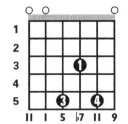
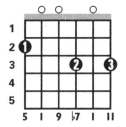

A13
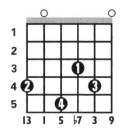
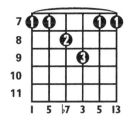
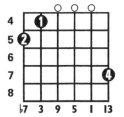

A Chords (Advanced)

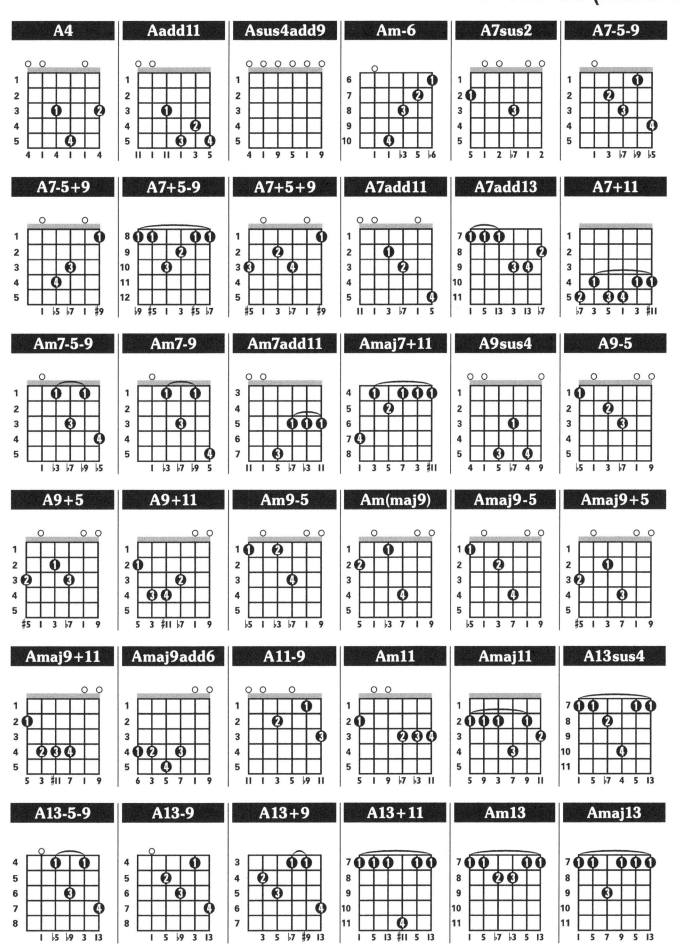

A# / B♭ Chords

B♭	B♭m	B♭7	B♭m7

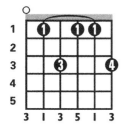 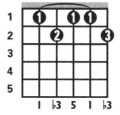 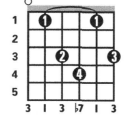 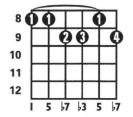

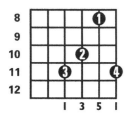 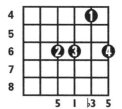 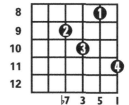 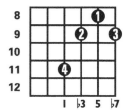

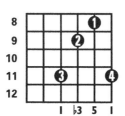 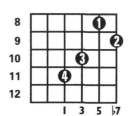 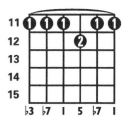

B♭5	B♭6	B♭m6	B♭maj7

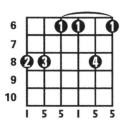 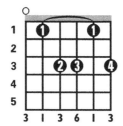 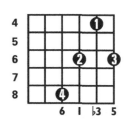 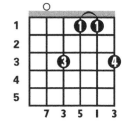

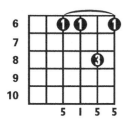 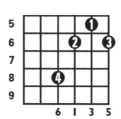 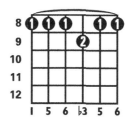 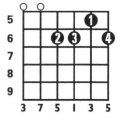

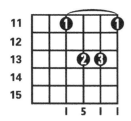 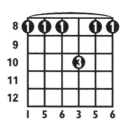 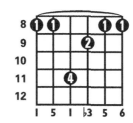 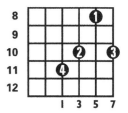

B♭°
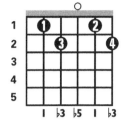
I ♭3 ♭5 I ♭3

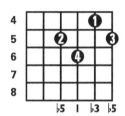
♭5 I ♭3 ♭5

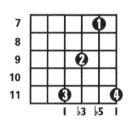
I ♭3 ♭5 I

B♭°7
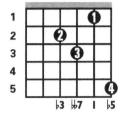
♭3 ♭♭7 I ♭5

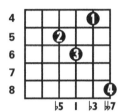
♭5 I ♭3 ♭♭7

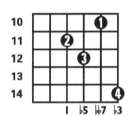
I ♭5 ♭♭7 ♭3

B♭-5
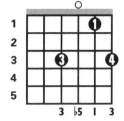
3 ♭5 I 3

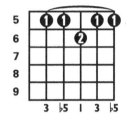
3 ♭5 I 3 ♭5

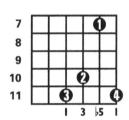
I 3 ♭5 I

B♭+
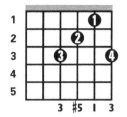
3 #5 I 3

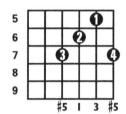
#5 I 3 #5

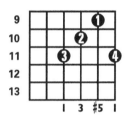
I 3 #5 I

B♭sus2
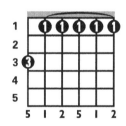
5 I 2 5 I 2

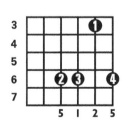
5 I 2 5

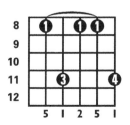
5 I 2 5 I

B♭sus4
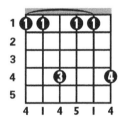
4 I 4 5 I 4

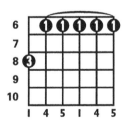
I 4 5 I 4 5

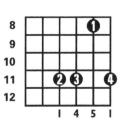
I 4 5 I

B♭7sus4
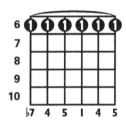
♭7 4 5 I 4 5

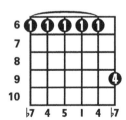
♭7 4 5 I 4 ♭7

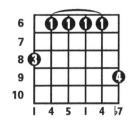
I 4 5 I 4 ♭7

B♭m7-5
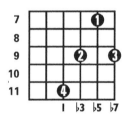
I ♭3 ♭5 ♭7

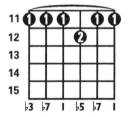
♭3 ♭7 I ♭5 ♭7 I

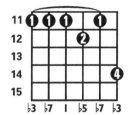
♭3 ♭7 I ♭5 ♭7 ♭3

A# / B♭ Chords

B♭add9

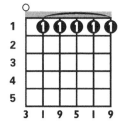
3 1 9 5 1 9

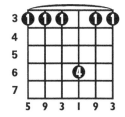
5 9 3 1 9 3

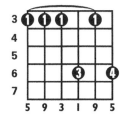
5 9 3 1 9 5

B♭madd9

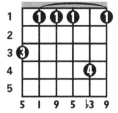
5 1 9 5 ♭3 9

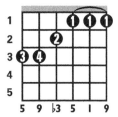
5 9 ♭3 5 1 9

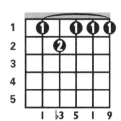
1 ♭3 5 1 9

B♭6add9

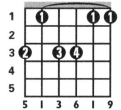
5 1 3 6 1 9

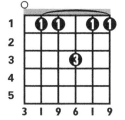
3 1 9 6 1 9

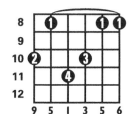
9 5 1 3 5 6

B♭m6add9

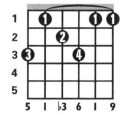
5 1 ♭3 6 1 9

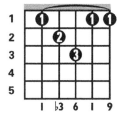
1 ♭3 6 1 9

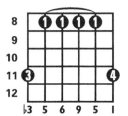
♭3 5 6 9 5 1

B♭7-5

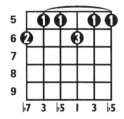
♭7 3 ♭5 1 3 ♭5

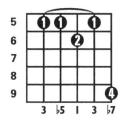
3 ♭5 1 3 ♭7

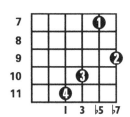
1 3 ♭5 ♭7

B♭7+5

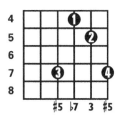
#5 ♭7 3 #5

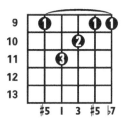
#5 1 3 #5 ♭7

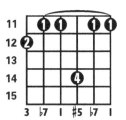
3 ♭7 1 #5 ♭7 1

B♭7-9

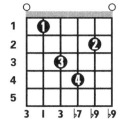
3 1 3 ♭7 ♭9 ♭9

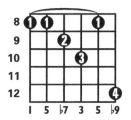
1 5 ♭7 3 5 ♭9

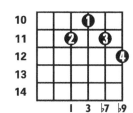
1 3 ♭7 ♭9

B♭7+9

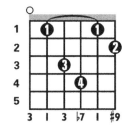
3 1 3 ♭7 1 #9

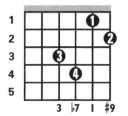
3 ♭7 1 #9

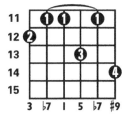
3 ♭7 1 5 ♭7 #9

64

B♭m(maj7)

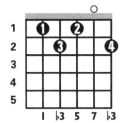

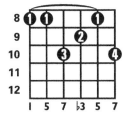

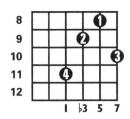

B♭maj7-5

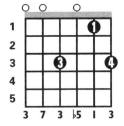

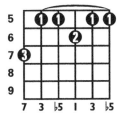

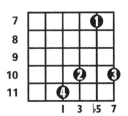

B♭maj7+5

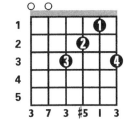

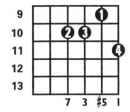

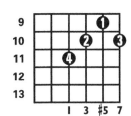

B♭9

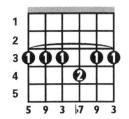

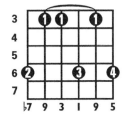

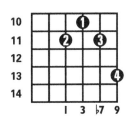

B♭m9

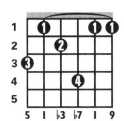

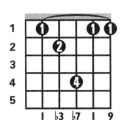

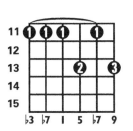

B♭11

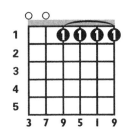

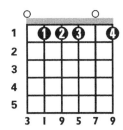

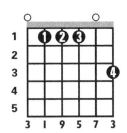

B♭maj9

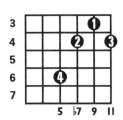

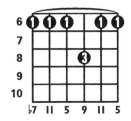

B♭13

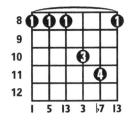

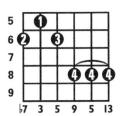

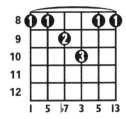

A# / B♭ Chords (Advanced)

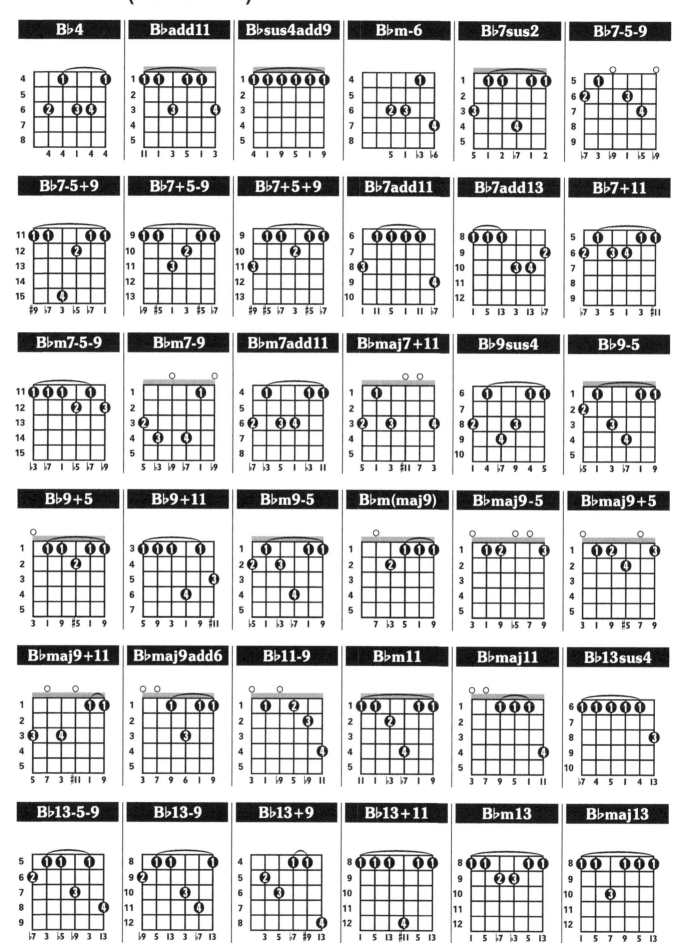

B Chords

B

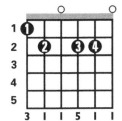

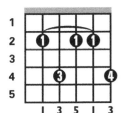

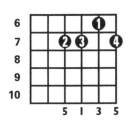

Bm

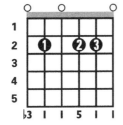

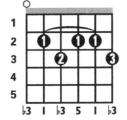

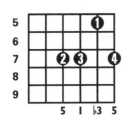

B7

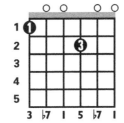

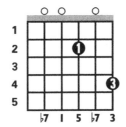

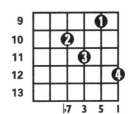

Bm7

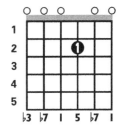

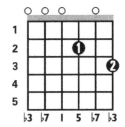

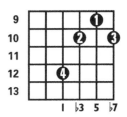

B5

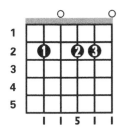

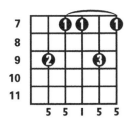

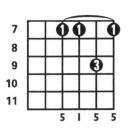

B6

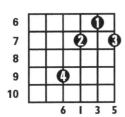

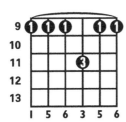

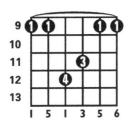

Bm6

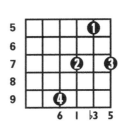

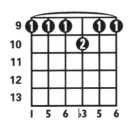

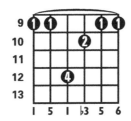

Bmaj7

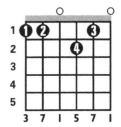

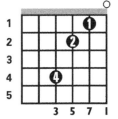

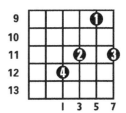

B Chords

B°	**B°7**	**B-5**	**B+**

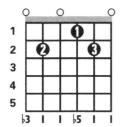 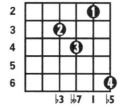 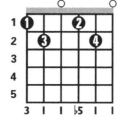 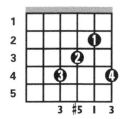

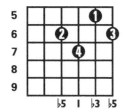 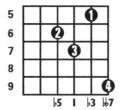 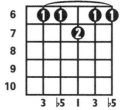 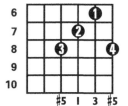

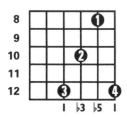 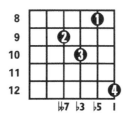 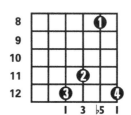 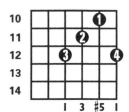

Bsus2	**Bsus4**	**B7sus4**	**Bm7-5**

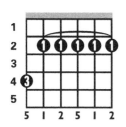 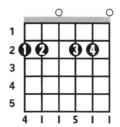 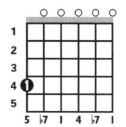 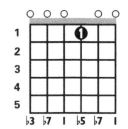

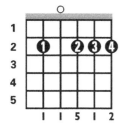 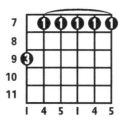 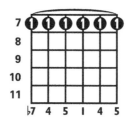 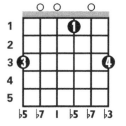

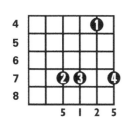 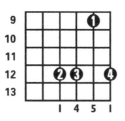 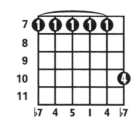 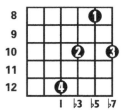

B Chords

Badd9
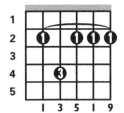
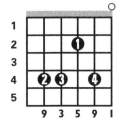
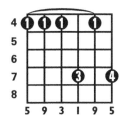

Bmadd9
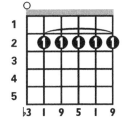
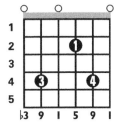
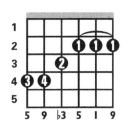

B6add9
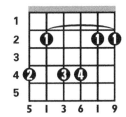
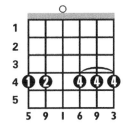
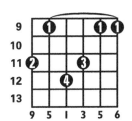

Bm6add9
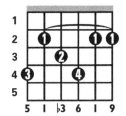
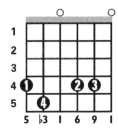
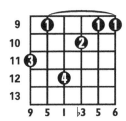

B7-5
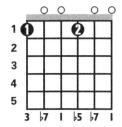
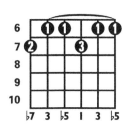
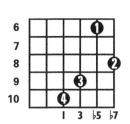

B7+5
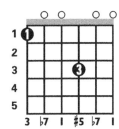
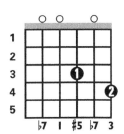
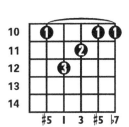

B7-9
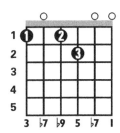
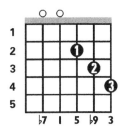
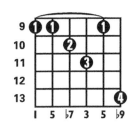

B7+9
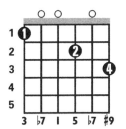
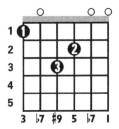
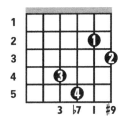

69

B Chords

Bm(maj7)
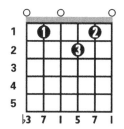
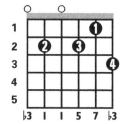
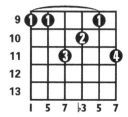

Bmaj7-5
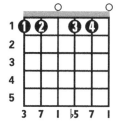
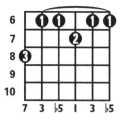
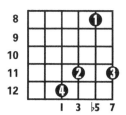

Bmaj7+5
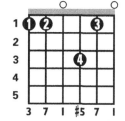
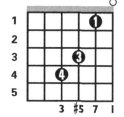
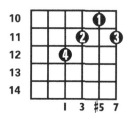

B9
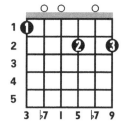
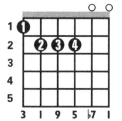
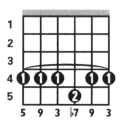

Bm9
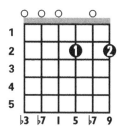
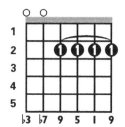
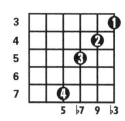

Bmaj9
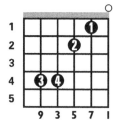
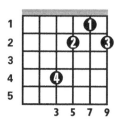
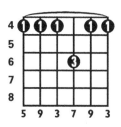

B11
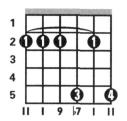
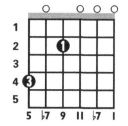
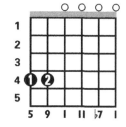

B13
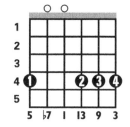
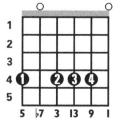
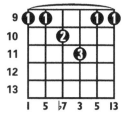

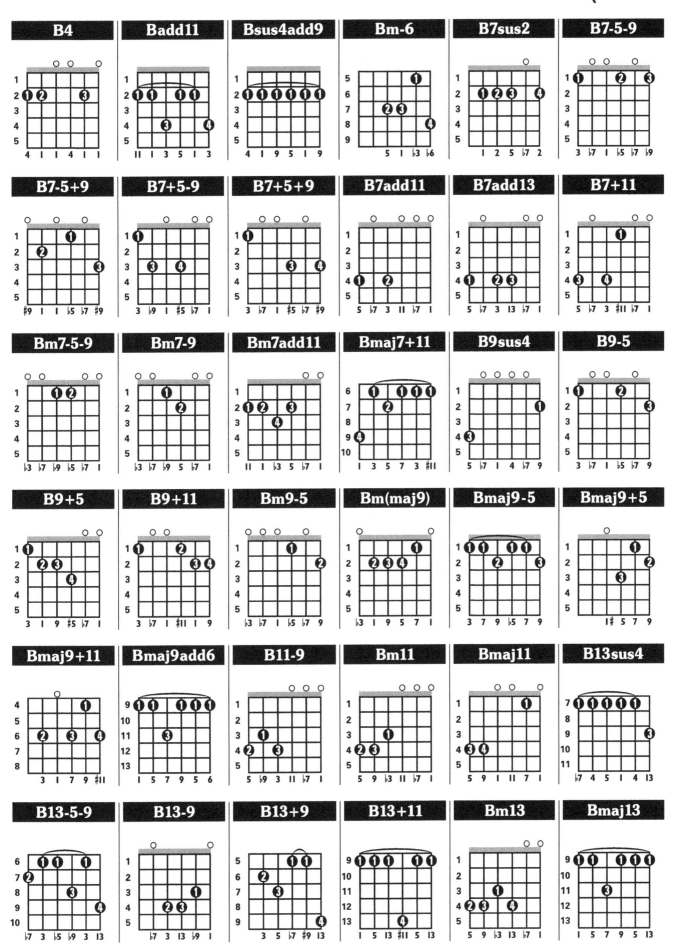

Major Slash Chords

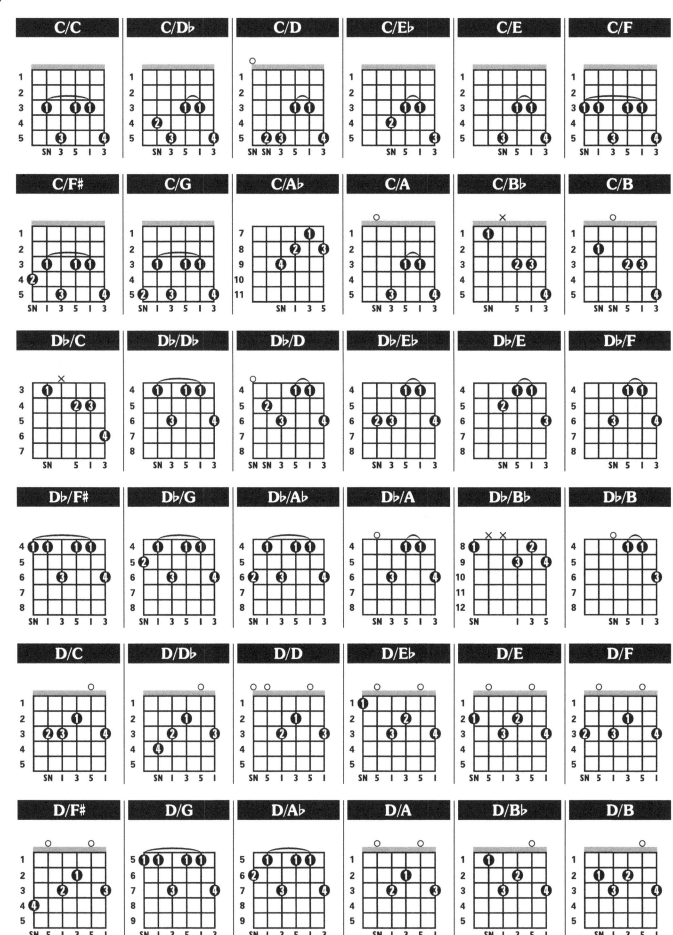

Major Slash Chords

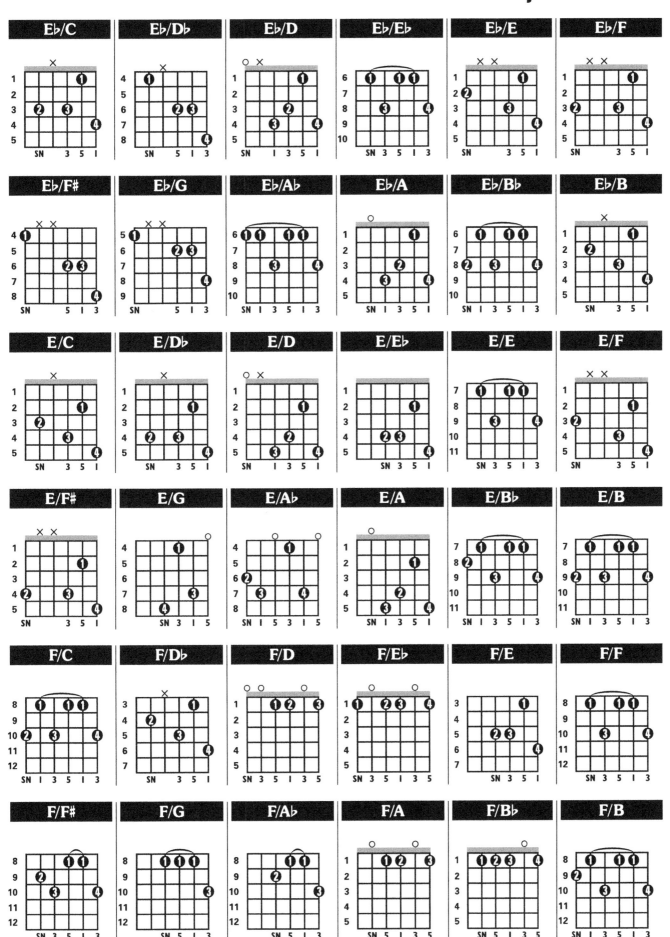

Major Slash Chords

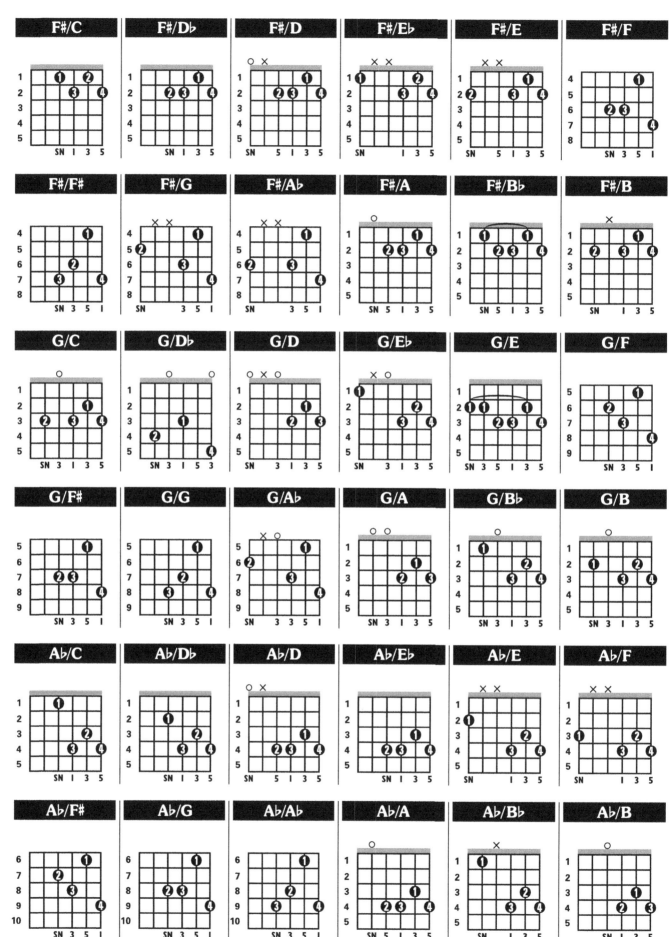

Major Slash Chords

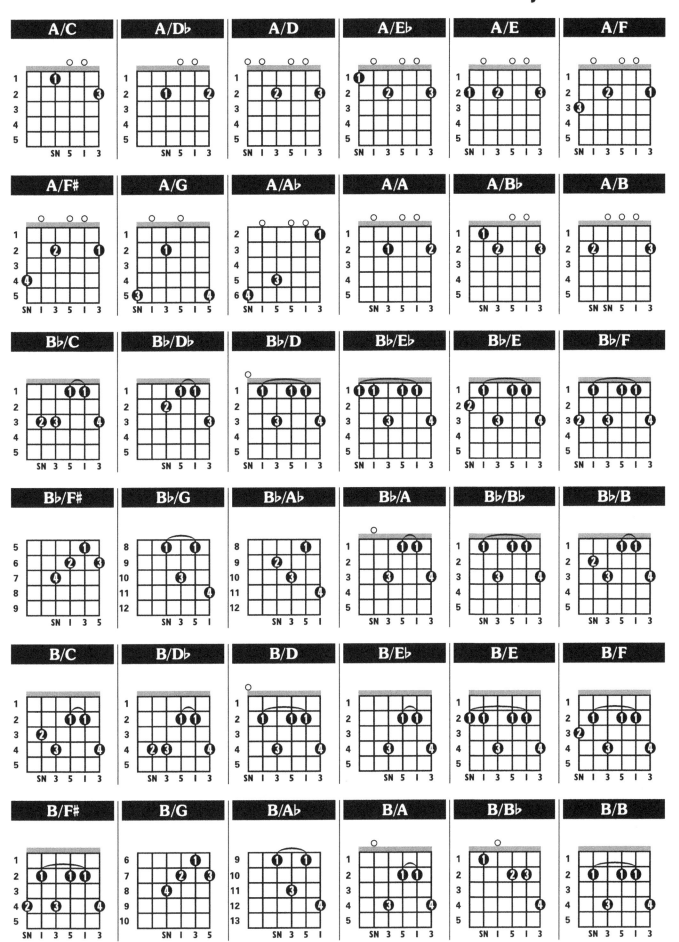

75

A Selection of Moveable Chord Shapes

Major

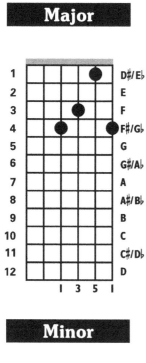

1	D#/Eb
2	E
3	F
4	F#/Gb
5	G
6	G#/Ab
7	A
8	A#/Bb
9	B
10	C
11	C#/Db
12	D

I 3 5 I

Major

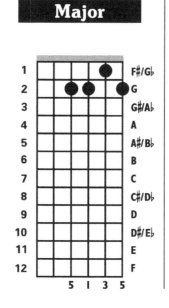

1	F#/Gb
2	G
3	G#/Ab
4	A
5	A#/Bb
6	B
7	C
8	C#/Db
9	D
10	D#/Eb
11	E
12	F

5 I 3 5

Major

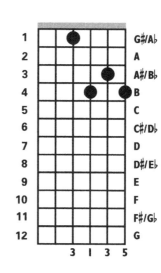

1	G#/Ab
2	A
3	A#/Bb
4	B
5	C
6	C#/Db
7	D
8	D#/Eb
9	E
10	F
11	F#/Gb
12	G

3 I 3 5

Major

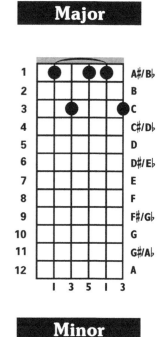

1	A#/Bb
2	B
3	C
4	C#/Db
5	D
6	D#/Eb
7	E
8	F
9	F#/Gb
10	G
11	G#/Ab
12	A

I 3 5 I 3

Minor

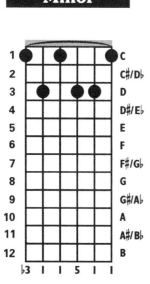

1	C
2	C#/Db
3	D
4	D#/Eb
5	E
6	F
7	F#/Gb
8	G
9	G#/Ab
10	A
11	A#/Bb
12	B

b3 I I 5 I I

Minor

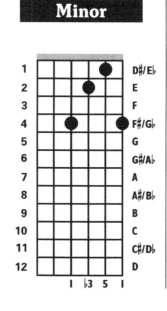

1	D#/Eb
2	E
3	F
4	F#/Gb
5	G
6	G#/Ab
7	A
8	A#/Bb
9	B
10	C
11	C#/Db
12	D

I b3 5 I

Minor

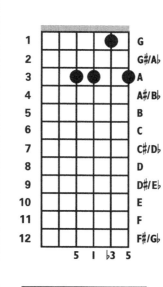

1	G
2	G#/Ab
3	A
4	A#/Bb
5	B
6	C
7	C#/Db
8	D
9	D#/Eb
10	E
11	F
12	F#/Gb

5 I b3 5

Minor

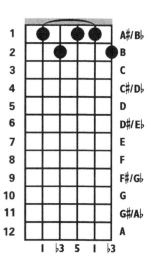

1	A#/Bb
2	B
3	C
4	C#/Db
5	D
6	D#/Eb
7	E
8	F
9	F#/Gb
10	G
11	G#/Ab
12	A

I b3 5 I b3

Seventh

1	D#/Eb
2	E
3	F
4	F#/Gb
5	G
6	G#/Ab
7	A
8	A#/Bb
9	B
10	C
11	C#/Db
12	D

I 5 b7 3 5 b7

Seventh

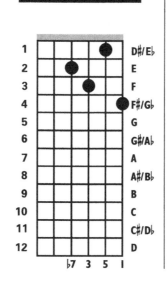

1	D#/Eb
2	E
3	F
4	F#/Gb
5	G
6	G#/Ab
7	A
8	A#/Bb
9	B
10	C
11	C#/Db
12	D

b7 3 5 I

Seventh

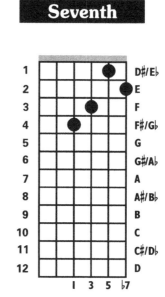

1	D#/Eb
2	E
3	F
4	F#/Gb
5	G
6	G#/Ab
7	A
8	A#/Bb
9	B
10	C
11	C#/Db
12	D

I 3 5 b7

Seventh

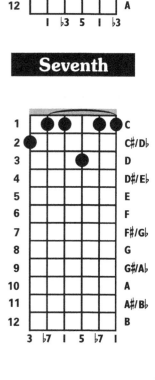

1	C
2	C#/Db
3	D
4	D#/Eb
5	E
6	F
7	F#/Gb
8	G
9	G#/Ab
10	A
11	A#/Bb
12	B

3 b7 I 5 b7 I

A Selection of Moveable Chord Shapes

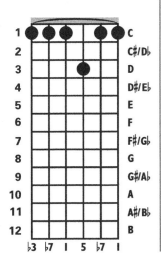

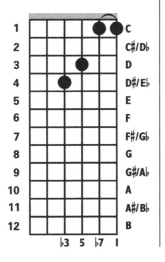

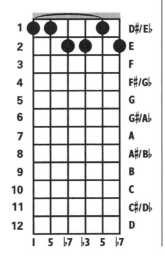

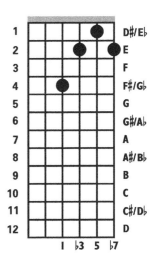

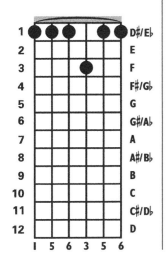

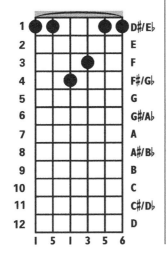

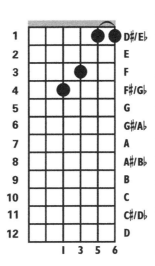

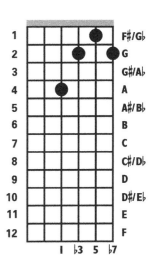

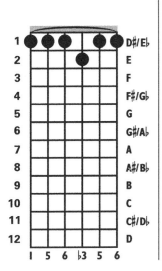

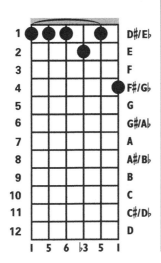

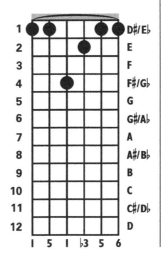

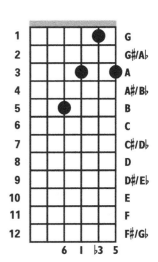

77

A Selection of Moveable Chord Shapes

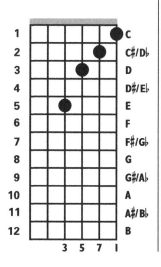

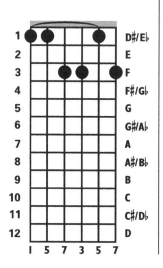

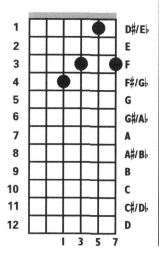

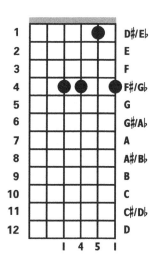

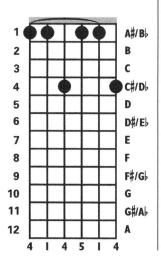

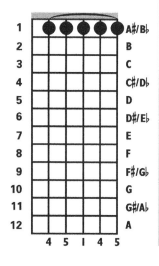

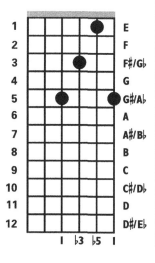

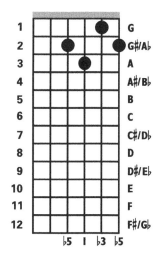

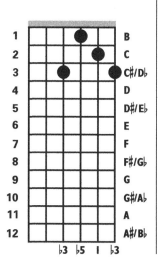

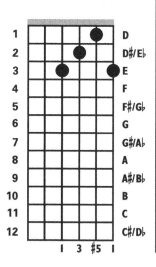

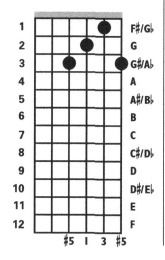

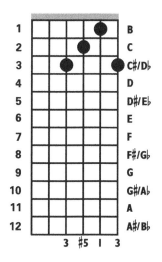

A Selection of Moveable Chord Shapes

Diminished Seventh
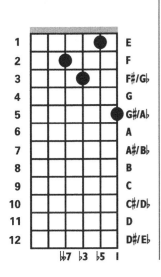

Diminished Seventh
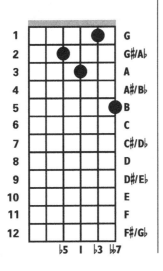

Fifth
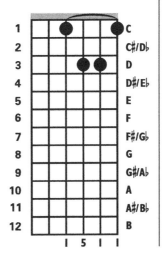

Fifth
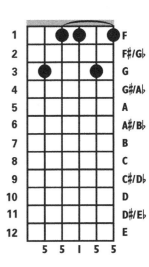

Seventh Suspended
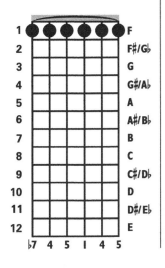

Added Ninth
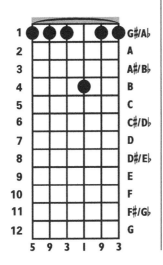

Added Ninth
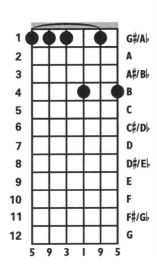

Ninth
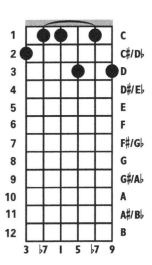

Minor Ninth
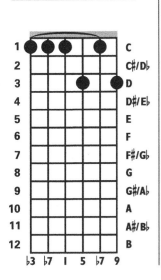

Major Ninth
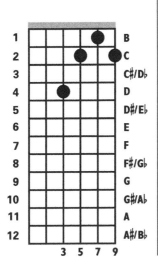

Eleventh
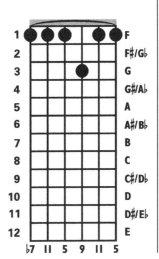

Thirteenth
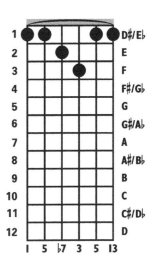

79

THE CITTERN & MANDOLIN FAMILY FACTFILE

Bandolim

Portuguese version of the mandolin. The bandolim features Preston-style tuners and a flatback, but still retains the standard GDAE tuning of its Italian counterpart. The teardrop shape is also more akin to the modern cittern-style instrument family, rather than the traditional Italian design of the bowl-back mandolin.

Cittern or Celtic Cittern

The modern celtic-style flatback cittern generally has five courses of strings and a variety of scale lengths of anything between 530mm/21 inches and 650mm/25½ inches. Confusingly, these are referred to as citterns by some luthiers and 5-string bouzoukis by others. Ultimately though, the nomenclature used by the different makers matters less than the scale length they employ on their particular instruments.

Of all the members of the mandolin/cittern family, the 10-course instrument has the least established standardized tuning, with players experimenting with various modal and mandolin-style configurations. Current popular tunings include: CGDAE, DGDAD, DGDAE, DGDGD, DADAD and EAEAE for long scales and GDADA, GDAEB, GDAEA, GCGCG, ADADA and ADGAD for short scales. Although the edges do get a little blurred when referring to scale lengths, as a rough guide, long scales can be up to 650mm/25½ and short scales between 530mm/21 and 580mm/23 inches. String selection also plays an important part in determining this as well.

English Guittar or English Guitar

The term English guittar is actually something of a misnomer. This 6-course, 10-stringed instrument should more accurately be classed as a form of cittern. It's popularity ran from the 1750s up until the 19th century where it was used as a parlour-style instrument. The only instruments you're likely to see today are luthier built reproduction models or antique instruments which have been restored. The tuning of the English guittar is set to a C major chord (C-E-G-C-E-G).

Arguably, the most famous maker of English guittars was John Preston of London whose watch-key style tuners can still be seen in operation today in instruments such as the Portuguese guitar and German waldzither. The waldzither in particular needs a special tuning wrench to tighten up or loosen the strings on the headstock. Musicians will generally wind their own strings for this style of instrument with a special string winder built for this purpose.

Halszither

A five-course guitar-shaped Swiss instrument that gained popularity at the end of the 19th and the start of the 20th century. The direct translation of halszither is 'cittern with a neck', to differentiate it from a standard tabletop zither. There are two dinstinct designs, the most popular being the Krienser named after the region in Switzerland where it was made. The second, the Toggenburger halszither conformed to more of standard cittern shape and featured 13 strings in 6 courses. Today, the halszither is very much a speciality instrument made to order by experienced luthiers.

If you are lucky enough to come across one, it's likely to be the Krienser model and not the Toggenburger which all but disappeared by the turn of the last century. Tuning for the Krienser is generally GDGBD (or open G Major) and CGCEG (or open C Major) for the Toggenburger.

Harzzither or Bergzither

The harzzither was a German cittern-style instrument, not dissimlar to its close relative, the waldzither. It was named after the Harz Mountain range in central Germany where it was made by local luthiers, who were very often musicians themselves. The stringing arrangement conforms more to the mandolin family than to it's cousin, the waldzither, with 8 strings set out in 4 courses. The tuning was GCEG (or open C Major). Traditionally, the harzzither is played with a plectrum to accompany a singer or as part of a folk music orchestra.

Irish Bouzouki

The history of the Irish bouzouki is relatively short in relation to other members of the mandolin family. It can be traced back to 1966 when Johnny Moynihan returned from a holiday in Greece with a traditional Greek bouzouki. He retuned it and began using it at gigs. However, the instrument we know today with it's flat back and cittern-style body shape was created for Moynihan by guitar luthier John Bailey who dispensed with the ribbed bowl back of the traditional Greek instrument. Today the bouzouki is well established in all styles of folk music and has begun making inroads into other musical genres including bluegrass, jazz and rock. The established tunings for the Irish bouzouki are GDAD (Irish), GDAE (fifths), ADAD (modal D) and GDGD (modal G). A bouzouki typical scale length is generally between 560-610mm or 22-24 inches. Colloquially, the bouzouki is often referred to as a *zouk*.

Laúd and Bandurria

A pair of Spanish folk instruments related to the mandolin/cittern family featuring a configuration of 12 strings in 6 courses tuned in 4ths. The laúd is tuned exactly one octave below its little sibling, with both forming an integral part of a traditional Spanish musical ensemble, together with the classical guitar. Because of its very short scale length, the bandurria tends to rely on melody playing, while its big brother, the laúd is more suitable for chodal work. Standard tuning for both instruments is G#-C#-F#-B-E-A. Several other family members of this group exist, but the bandurria and laud are by far the most widely used in today's Spanish folk music.

Mandobass

A very rare beast, even in its hey-day when Gibson produced these leviathans of the mandolin family as a direct replacement for the double bass. The tuning, like the upright or electric bass, is EADG.

Mandocello

As the name suggests, the mandocello takes its name and tuning from another member of the violin family, the cello. The tuning is pitched one octave below that of the mandola (CGDA), although it's not uncommon to string the instrument with lighter gauge strings and tune it like an Irish bouzouki or octave mandolin/mandola. In theory it's possible to tune down an Irish bouzouki or octave mandolin to CGDA, but the additional strain on the neck and body can cause structural problems. The heavier strings can also cause rattling in the lower courses. The mandocello has a scale length of between 630-660mm or 24¾-26 inches.

Mandola or Tenor Mandola

The mandola, as it's known in North America or tenor mandola in the United Kingdom, Ireland and Europe, takes its tuning directly from the viola (CGDA). It's also referred to in some circles as the alto mandola, reflecting the musical difference between it and the higher pitched *soprano* mandolin which is tuned GDAE (or a fifth higher). The scale length of a typical mandola is approximately 420mm or 16½ inches. Like other members of the mandolin family, the mandola is most popularly used within the many strands of European and North American folk music.

Mandolin

The mandolin comes in a bewildering array of different styles and constructional configurations, with the only constant being its traditional GDAE tuning in fifths. Its antecedents can be traced back as far as 15,000 B.C. and can be seen in its earliest forms in cave paintings. A typical mandolin has a scale of between 330mm and 370mm or 13-14½ inches.

The Neopolitan round or bowl-back style is mainly used in the classical repetoire. The bowl-back style we know today, though, can more accurately be attributed to the Italian Vinaccia family of luthiers from Naples. An existing example from 1744 of the family's work can be seen at the Conservatoire Royal de Musique in Brussels. Another fine example is on display at London's Victoria & Albert Museum. Although less common than other styles of mando, the Neopolitan is still popular today.

The F-Style or Florentine style mando was originally designed and built by New York born Orville H. Gibson. In 1902 a group of businessmen bought Gibson's patent and set themselves up as the Gibson Mandolin-Guitar Company. Gibson himself was originally employed as a consultant, gaining partnership status in 1915. The F-style is easily recognizable by its ornamental body scroll and violin-style f holes. Although not exclusively so, its popularity lies in bluegrass music where the sound is able to cut through and compete with other larger bodied instruments like the guitar and banjo.

The pear-shaped A-Style again is a Gibson design and can be found in a variety of music including folk, classical and bluegrass. It generally doesn't have quite the projection of the F-style, but has remained one of the popular standard designs to this day.

Celtic flatbacks are primarily used in folk music because of their rich tone, volume and sustaining qualities. They generally come with oval or round soundholes and make an ideal companion for other instruments such as the guitar and Irish bouzouki. Because of their long sustain, they're not really suitable for bluegrass music which requires a quick attack and rapidly decaying 'chop' sound.

Electric solid body and semi-acoustic mandolins are also common today. These have found their way into rock and other styles of music and come in single or double course versions. 5-String electric and acoustic mandolins are also becoming popular because of the additional lower course and are generally tuned CGDAE.

Octave Mandolin or Octave Mandola
The naming conventions on both sides of the Atlantic differ in much the same way as with the mandola or tenor mandola, with the term octave mandolin being used in North America and octave mandola in the UK, Ireland and Europe. As the name implies, the octave mandolin is pitched exactly one octave below the standard mandolin. The scale length can vary quite a bit from 500mm up to something as long as 600mm (19¾ to 23½ inches).

Piccolo or Sopranino Mandolin
A specialist instrument tuned exactly one octave above the mandola (CGDA) and only available from independent luthiers. The scale length is around 240mm or 9½ inches. As with other members of the mandolin family, the piccolo mando was created as a direct musical relation of the piccolo or sopranino violin.

Portuguese Guitar or Guitarra Portuguesa
The Portuguese guitar is a 12-string double course instrument used mainly within the confines of *Fado* music. The instrument's historical links can be traced back to the English Guittar and the Renaissance cittern, although there is still considerable debate about the specific parentage. This heritage was very apparent up until the end of the World War II, when the Portuguese guitar employed the same C-E-G-C-E-G *Natural* tuning as its English ancestor. Today, this has all but died out, with musician's opting for the current regional tunings associated with the two models of guitarra.

On the design front, there are two distinct designs with their own traditional regional tunings. Firstly, the Coimbra with its teardrop headstock protuberance and 470-490mm scale length tuned C-G-A-D-G-A. Secondly, the Lisboa or Lisbon guitarra, featuring a violin-like scroll on the headstock, a narrower neck/fingerboard arrangement and a shorter scale length of 440 or 458mm. The instrument is pitched D-A-B-E-A-B and is particularly associated with the accompaniment of *Fado* singing. Both forms include octave strings on the lowest three courses. Sound-wise, the Coimbra guitar has a fuller timbre with more bass response, while the Lisboa has more of a ringing tone. Different shaped *unhas* or finger and thumb picks are also employed by the two instruments. The Coimbra being rounded at the top like a fingertip as opposed to the Lisboa's much squarer corners, each producing its own very distinct sound and associated technique.

Simple Pronunciation Guide:
Coimbra: *Queem-brah*
Lisboa: *leezh-boa (with a soft 'g' sound on the 's')*
Unha (singular) / Unhas (plural): oon-yah / *oon-yas*

Traditionally, a picking technique called *dedillo* (or *dedilho*) is employed by musicians utilising only the index finger and thumb.

Tricordia or Mandriola
A triple course mandolin from Mexico (tricordia) and Europe (mandriola). The difference between the two being the use of octave strings in the European instrument as opposed to the tricordias unison pairings. The sound is a lot fuller than the standard double-course mandolin with more of a shimmering timbre to it.

Waldzither (or Forest Zither)
A traditional German 9-string/5-course cittern tuned to an open C chord (CGCEG) and featuring a scale length of between 430mm and 460mm. Two distinct styles exist - the first being the earlier Thüringen instrument with its regular mandolin/guitar style tuners. The second being a later 1900 design patented by German company C. H. Böhm with its drum/piano key-style tuners, which closely resemble the watch-key tuners used on the Portuguese guitar.

The most popular member of the Waldzither family is the tenor, but other sizes also exist including the piccolo (an octave higher, also tuned CGCEG), the descant or *diskant* (tuned GDGBD) and the bass (AEAC#E). An alternative tuning for the tenor features an open D Major chord (DADF#A) - a whole tone higher than the standard open C.

The following list of cittern and mandolin family members includes a selection of some of the more widely used standard and popular tunings. The tuning arrangement in the right hand column lists the notes from right to left (or low to high).

The Cittern & Mandolin Family Tunings

Bandolim	GDAE
Bandurria	G#C#F#BEA
Cittern (Longscale Fifths Tuning)	CGDAE
Cittern (Longscale Irish Tuning)	DGDAD
Cittern (Longscale Mandocello+Tuning)	CGDAD
Cittern (Longscale Mandolin+Tuning)	DGDAE
Cittern (Longscale Modal A Tuning)	EAEAE
Cittern (Longscale Modal C Tuning)	CGCGC
Cittern (Longscale Modal D Tuning)	DADAD
Cittern (Longscale Modal F Tuning)	CFCFC
Cittern (Longscale Modal G Tuning)	DGDGD
Cittern (Longscale Asus4 Tuning)	DAEAE
Cittern (Shortscale Fifths Tuning)	GDAEB
Cittern (Shortscale Mandolin+Tuning)	GDAEA
Cittern (Shortscale Modal C Tuning)	GCGCG
Cittern (Shortscale Modal D Tuning)	ADADA
Cittern (Shortscale Modal F Tuning)	FCFCF
Cittern (Shortscale Modal G Tuning)	GDGDG
Cittern (Shortscale Dsus4 Tuning)	GDADA
English Guittar or English Guitar	CEGCEG
Greek Bouzouki	CFAD
Halszither (Krienser)	GDGBD
Halszither (Toggenburger)	CGCEG
Harzzither	GCEG
Irish Bouzouki (Fifths Tuning)	GDAE
Irish Bouzouki (Irish Tuning)	GDAD
Irish Bouzouki (Modal D Tuning)	ADAD
Irish Bouzouki (Modal G Tuning)	GDGD
Laúd(Cuban Tuning)	DF#BEAD
Laúd(Filipino Tuning)	F#BEADG
Laúd (Spanish Tuning)	G#C#F#BEA
Mandobass	EADG
Mandocello	GCDA
Mandola or Tenor Mandola	CGDA
Mandolin	GDAE
Octave Mandolin or Octave Mandola	GDAE
Piccolo or Soprano Mandolin	CGDA
Portuguese Guitar (Coimbra Tuning)	CGADGA
Portuguese Guitar (Lisboa Tuning)	DABEAB
Portuguese Guitar (Natural Tuning)	CEGCEG
Waldzither (Bass in A Major)	AEAC#E
Waldzither (Descant in G Major)	GDGBD
Waldzither (Piccolo in C Major)	CGCEG
Waldzither (Tenor in Standard C Major)	CGCEG
Waldzither (Tenor in D Major)	DADF#A

ALTERNATIVE CHORD NAMES

C	**CM** or **Cmaj**
Cm	**Cmin** or **C-**
C-5	**C-5** or **C(♭5)**
C°	**Cdim**
C4	**Csus4(no 5th)** or **Csus(no 5th)**
C5	**C Power Chord** or **C(no 3rd)**
Csus2	**C(sus2)** or **C2**
Csus4	**Csus** or **C(sus4)**
Csus4add9	**Csus(add9)**
C+	**Caug, C+5** or **C(#5)**
C6	**CM6** or **CMaj6**
Cadd9	**Cadd2**
Cm6	**C-6** or **Cmin6**
Cmadd9	**Cmadd2** or **C-(add9)**
C6add9	**C6/9, C$^6_9$** or **CMaj6(add9)**
Cm6add9	**Cm6/9** or **Cm$^6_9$**
C°7	**Cdim7**
C7	**Cdom**
C7sus2	**C7(sus2)**
C7sus4	**C7sus, C7(sus4)** or **Csus11**
C7-5	**C7♭5**
C7+5	**C7+** or **C7#5**
C7-9	**C7♭9** or **C7(add♭9)**
C7+9	**C7#9** or **C7(add#9)**
C7-5-9	**C7♭5♭9**
C7+5-9	**C7#5♭9**
C7+5+9	**C7#5#9**
C7add11	**C7/11** or **C$^7_{11}$**
C7+11	**C7#11**
Cm7	**C-7, Cmi7** or **Cmin7**
Cm7-5	**Cm7♭5, C-7-5** or **C∅**
Cm7-5-9	**Cm7♭5♭9**
Cm7-9	**Cm7♭9**
Cm7add11	**Cm**
Cm(maj7)	**Cm#7, CM7-5, CmM7** or **C-△**
Cmaj7	**CM7** or **C△(Delta)**
Cmaj7-5	**CM7-5, C△♭5** or **Cmaj7♭5**
Cmaj7+5	**CM7+5, C△5+** or **Cmaj7#11**
Cmaj7+11	**CM7+11, C△+#11** or **Cmaj7#11**
C9	**C7(add9)**
C9sus4	**C9sus** or **C9(sus4)**
C9-5	**C9♭5**
C9+5	**C9#5**
C9+11	**C9#11**
Cm9	**C-9** or **Cmin9**
Cm9-5	**Cm9♭5**
Cm(maj9)	**Cm9(maj7), CmM9** or **Cm(addM9)**
Cmaj9	**CM9, Cmaj7(add9), C△9** or **CM7(add9)**
Cmaj9-5	**CM9-5, Cmaj9♭5, C△9♭5** or **CM9♭5**
Cmaj9+5	**CM9+5, Cmaj9#5, C△9#5**
Cmaj9add6	**CM9add6** or **C△9add6**
Cmaj9+11	**CM9+11, Cmaj9#11, C△9#11** or **CM9#11**
C11	**C7(add11)**
C11-9	**C11♭9**
Cm11	**C-11** or **Cmin11**
Cmaj11	**CM11, Cmaj7(add11), C△11, CM7(add11)**
C13	**C7/6(no 9th)** or **C7(add13)**
C13sus4	**C13sus** or **C13(sus4)**
C13-5-9	**C13♭5♭9**
C13-9	**C13♭9**
C13+9	**C13#9**
C13+11	**C13#11** or **C13aug11**

Cm13	**C-13** or **Cmin13**
Cmaj13	**CM13, Cmaj7(add13),** **C△13** or **CM7(add13)**

M	**major**
m	**minor**
-	**minor**
dim	**diminished**
°	**diminished**
∅	**half diminished**
sus	**suspended**
aug	**augmented**
+	**augmented**
add	**added**
dom	**dominant**
△	**delta /major seventh**
Q(3)	**quartal / double fourth**
#	**sharp**
×	**double sharp**
♭	**flat**
♭♭	**double flat**

Do	**Spanish for C**
Dó	**Portuguese for C**
Re	**Spanish for D**
Ré	**Portuguese for D**
Mi	**Spanish & Portuguese for E**
Fa	**Spanish & Portuguese for F**
So	**Spanish for G**
Sol	**Portuguese for G**
La	**Spanish for A**
Lá	**Portuguese for A**
Si	**Spanish & Portuguese for B**
H	**German for B**

English Tonic Sol-fa

Do	**C**
Re	**D**
Me	**E**
Fa	**F**
Sol	**G**
La	**A**
Ti	**B**

The majority of music books will use the chords featured in the first column (on the far left and top right), but should you come across alternatives, consult this guide for other naming conventions.

The list above includes most of the symbols and abbreviations that you're likely to encounter in the majority of music books.

NOTES

NOTES

NOTES

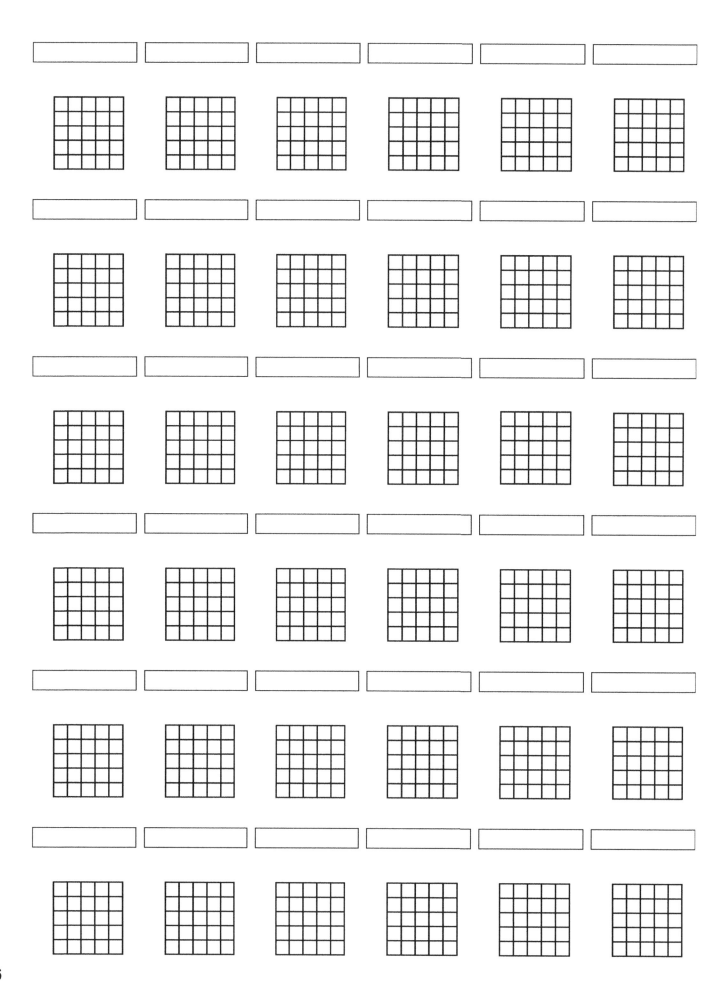

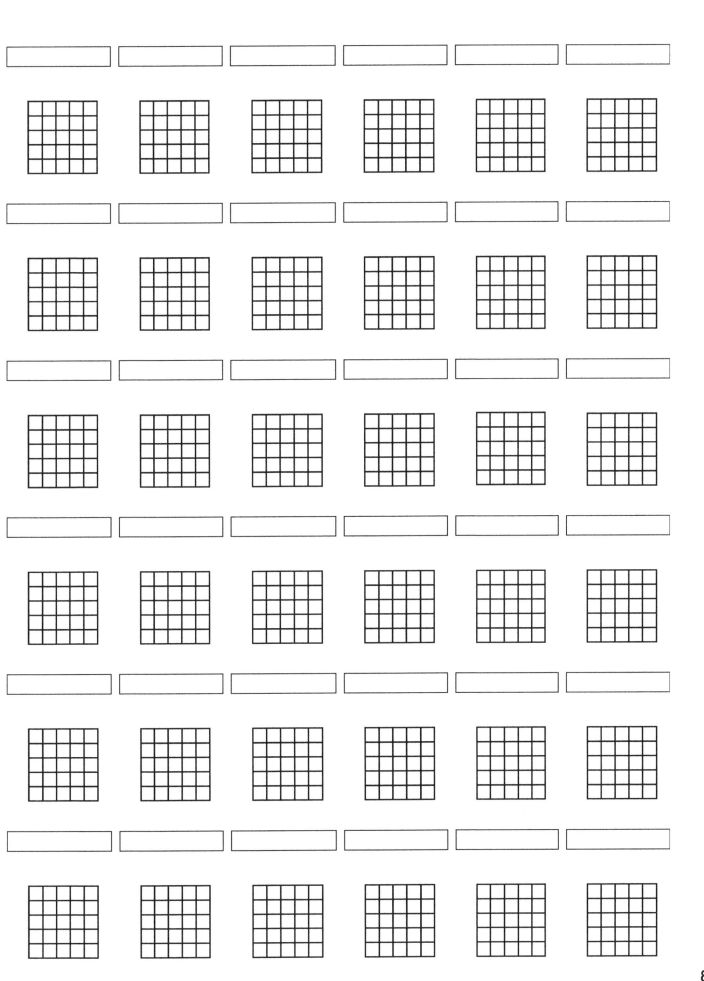

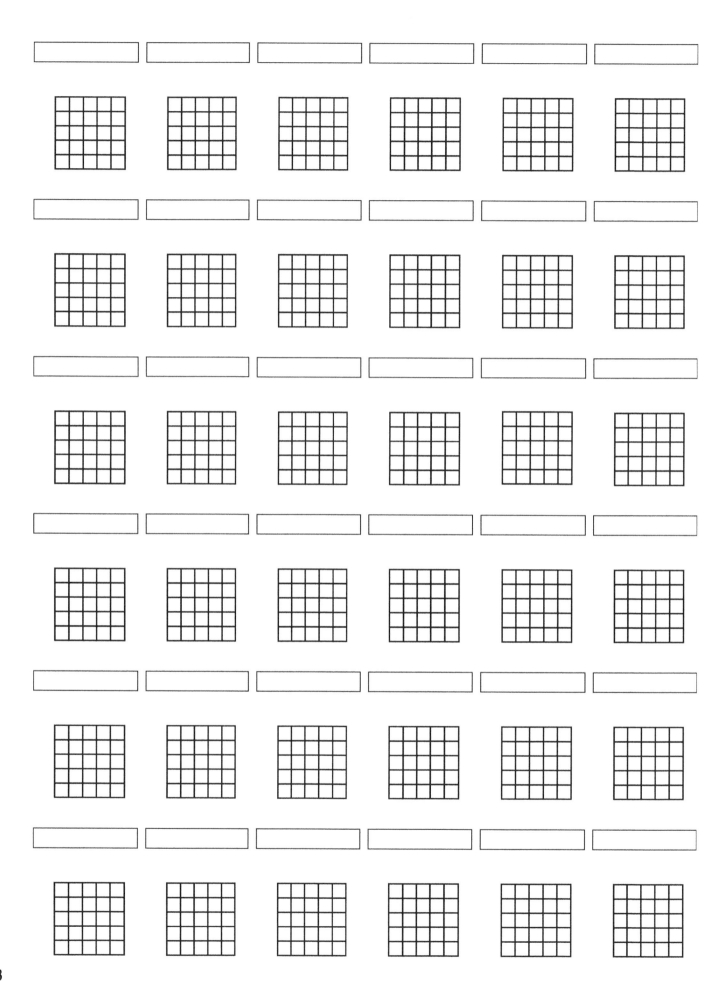

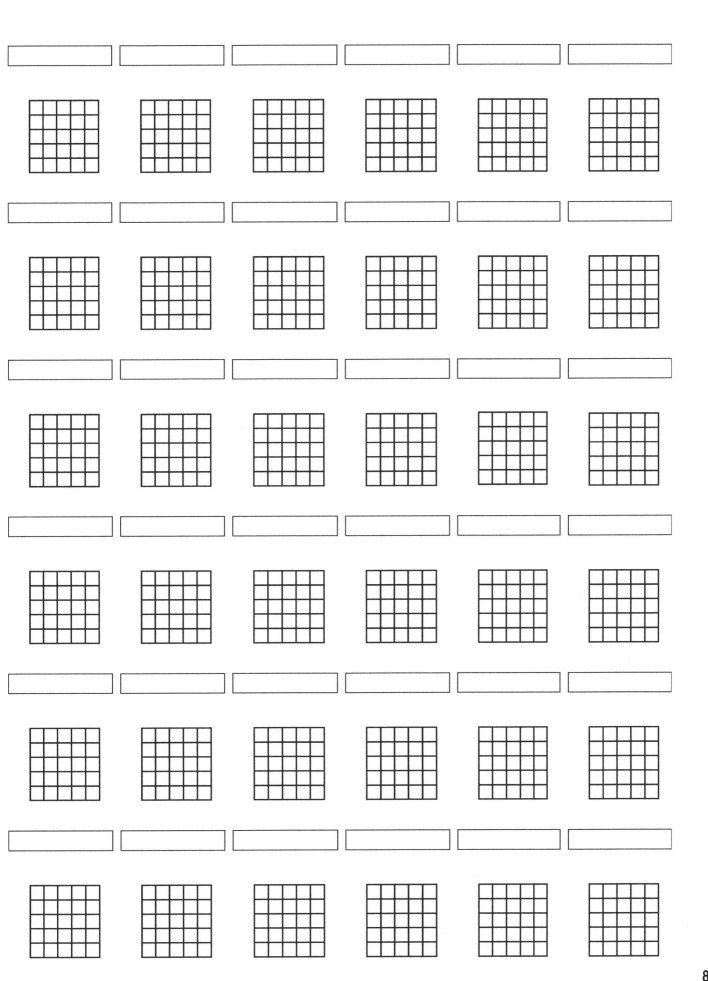

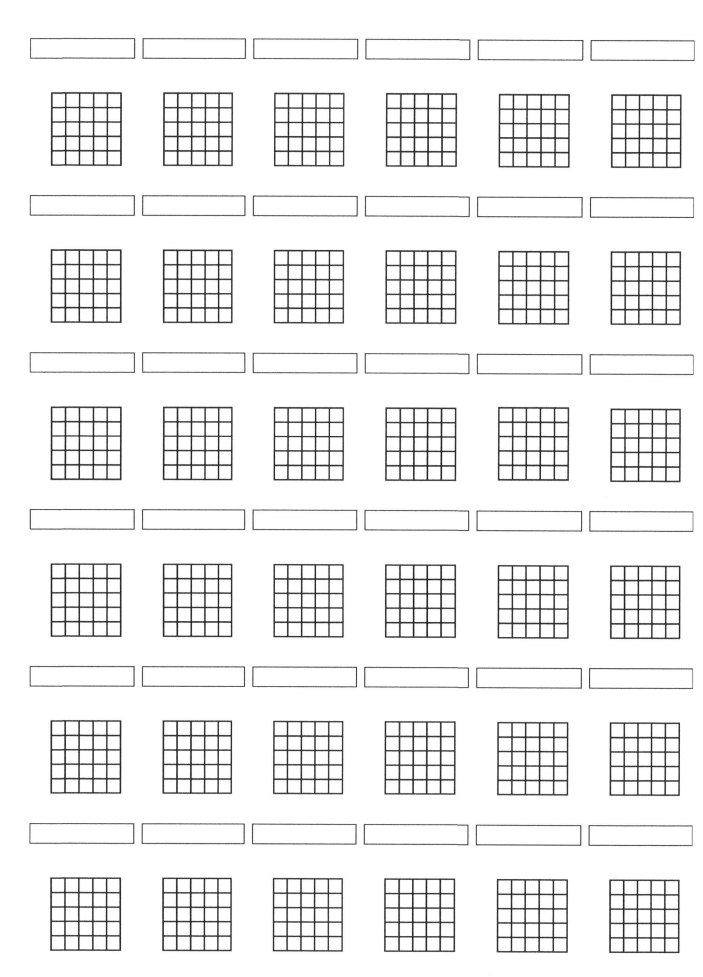

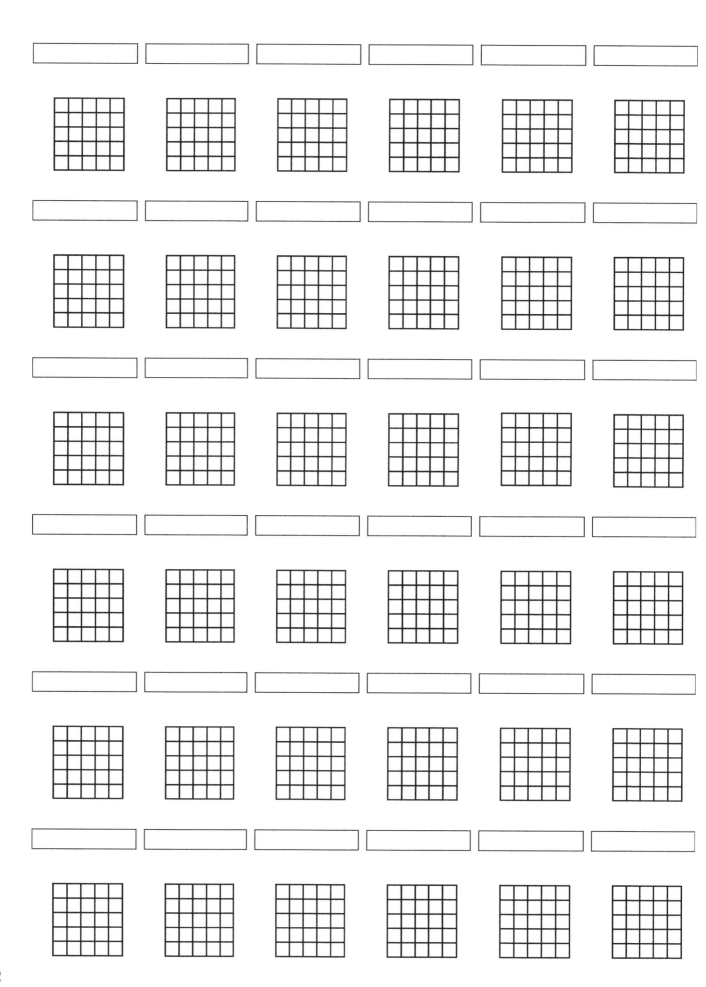

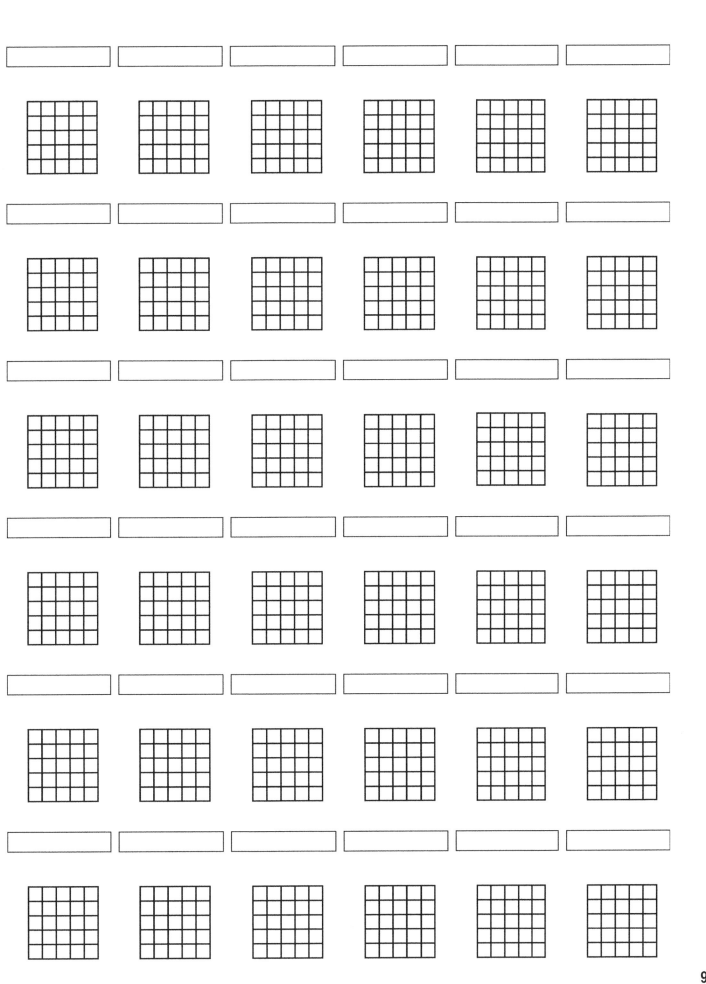

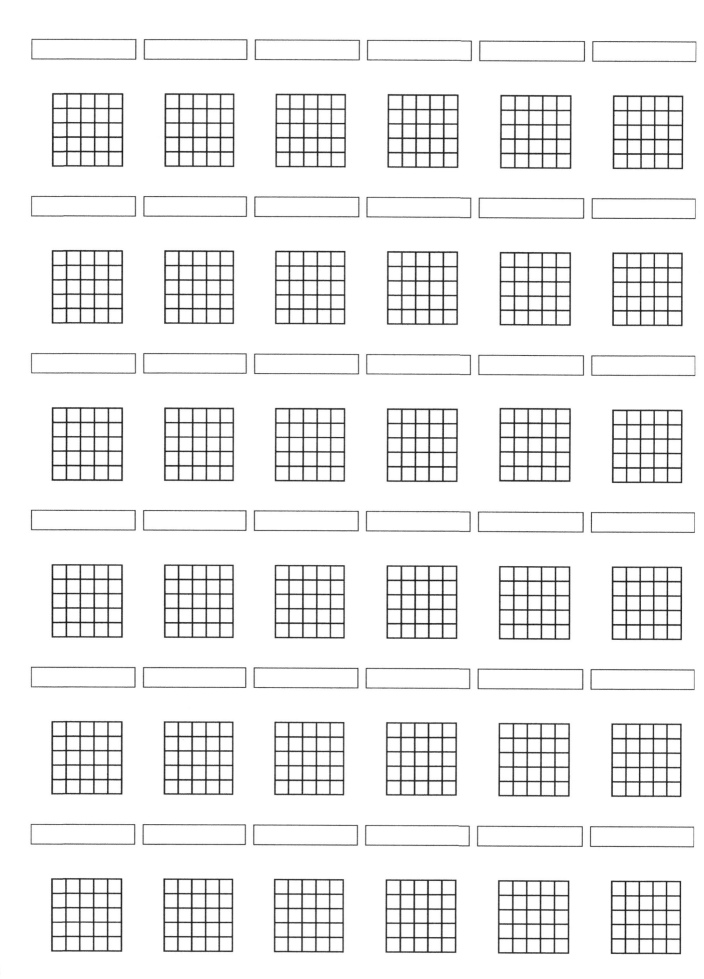

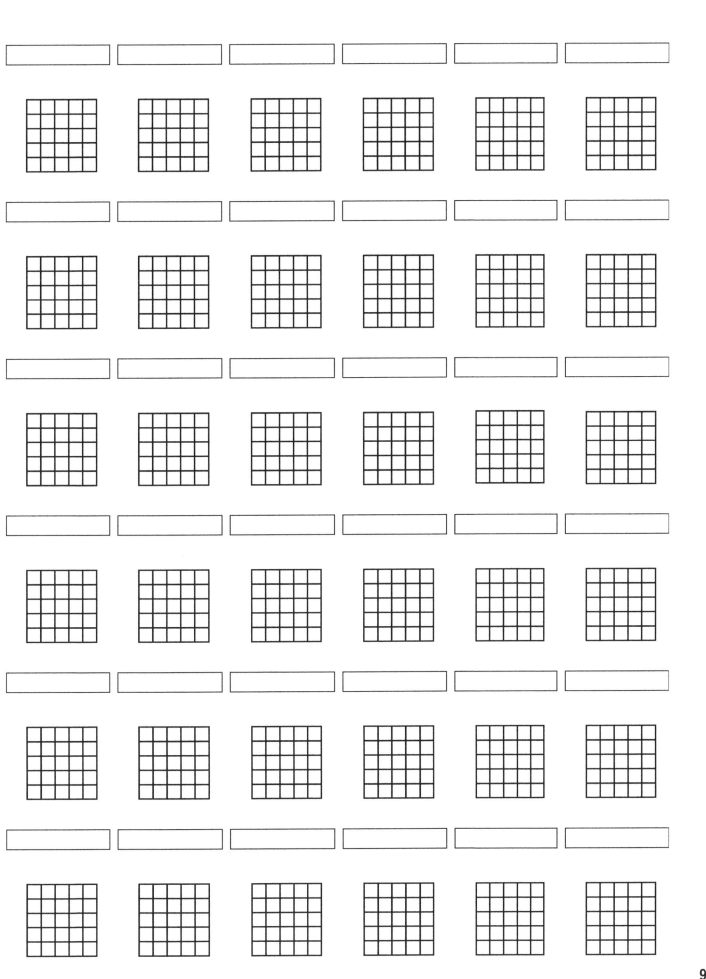

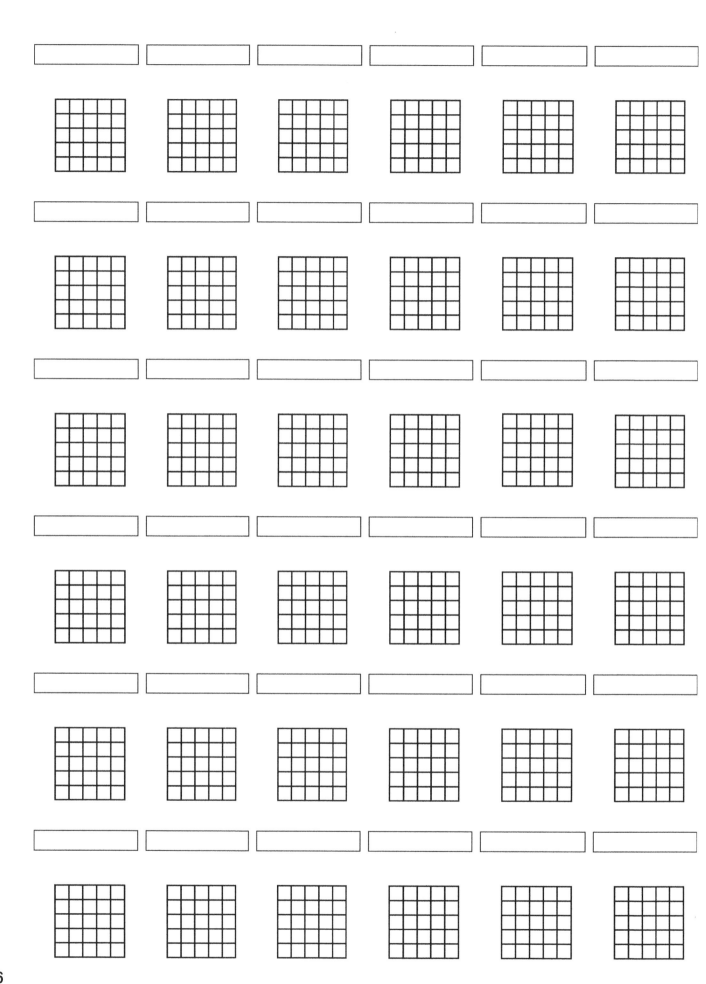

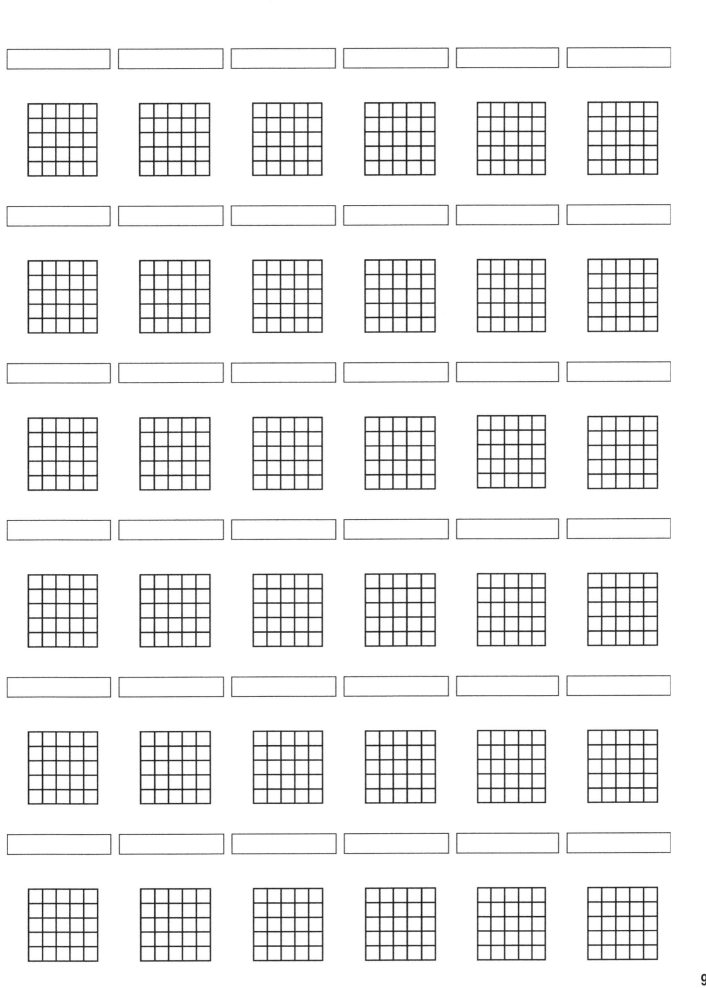

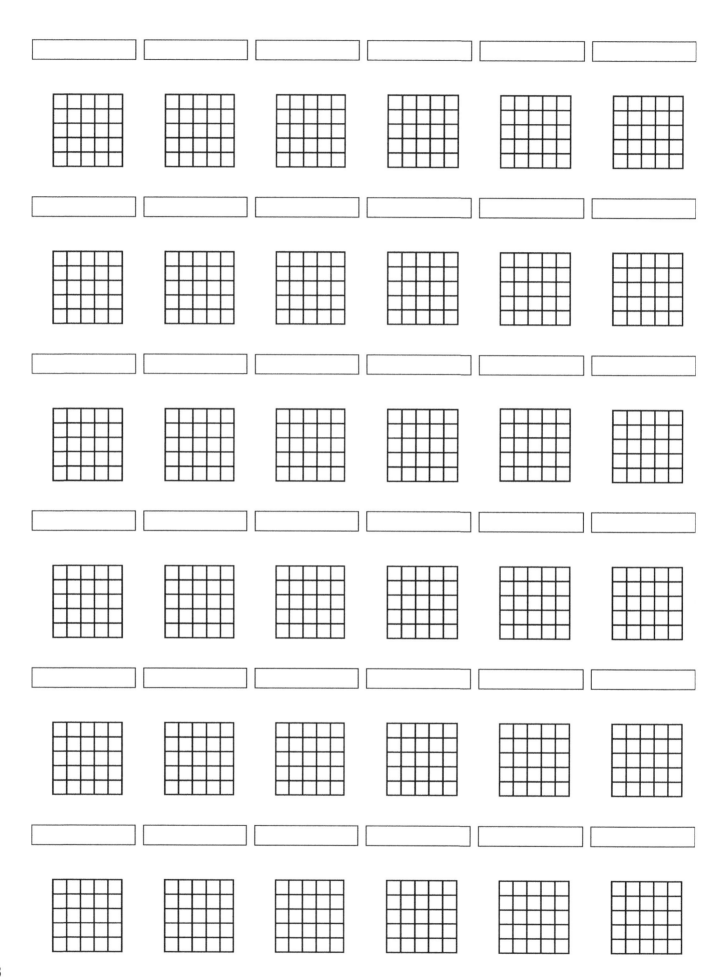

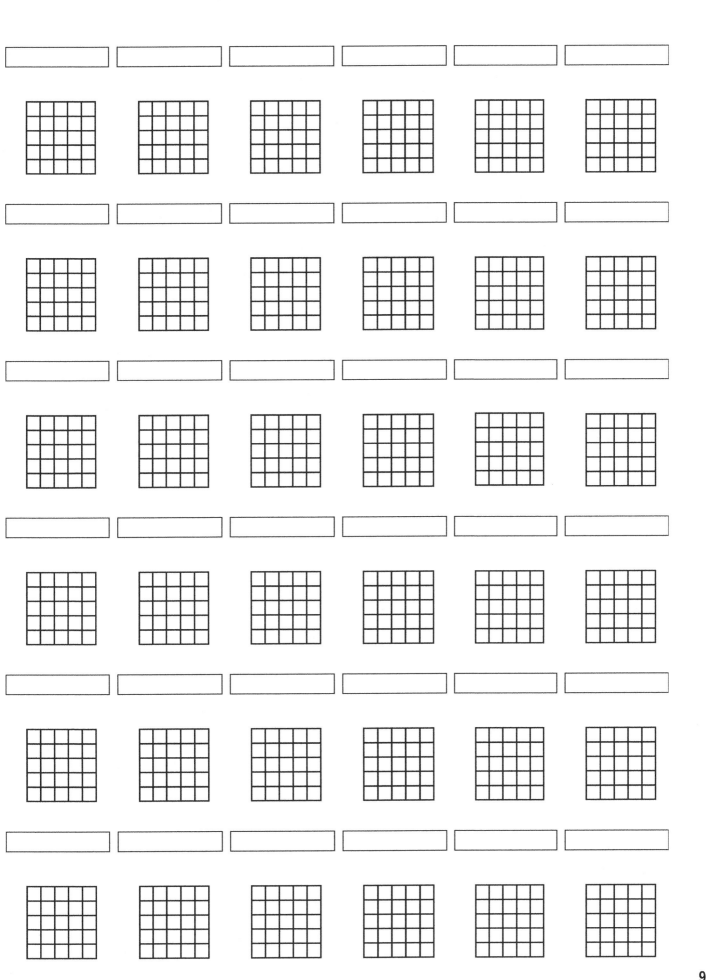

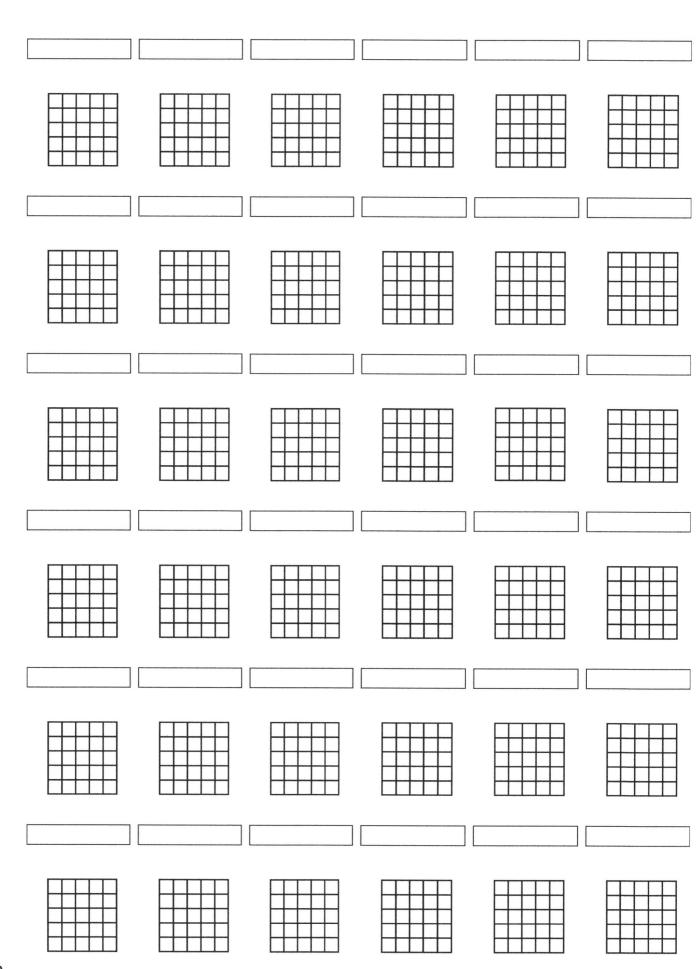

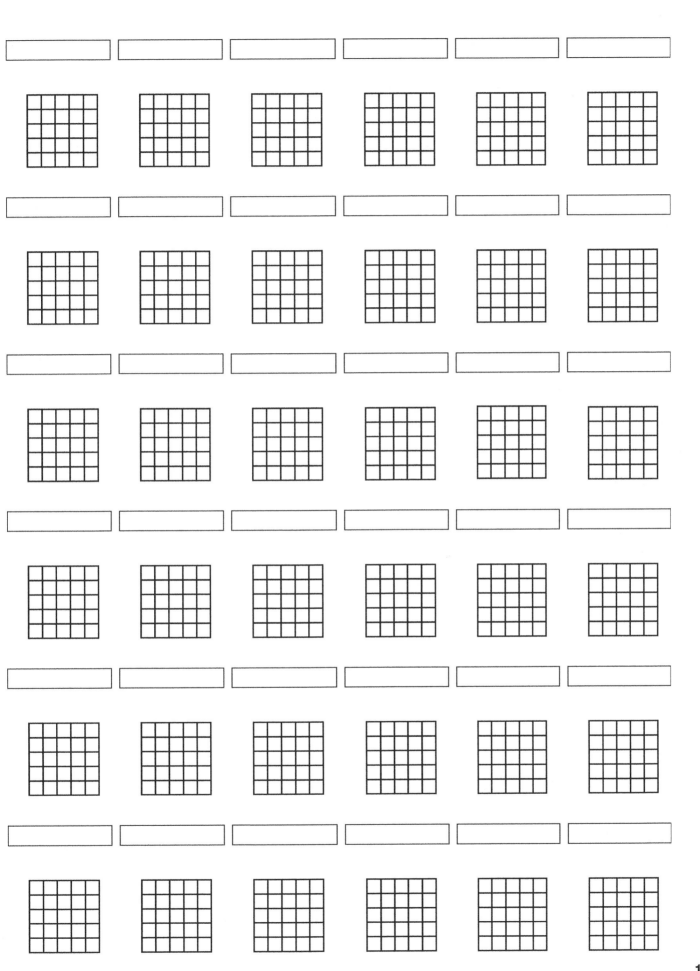

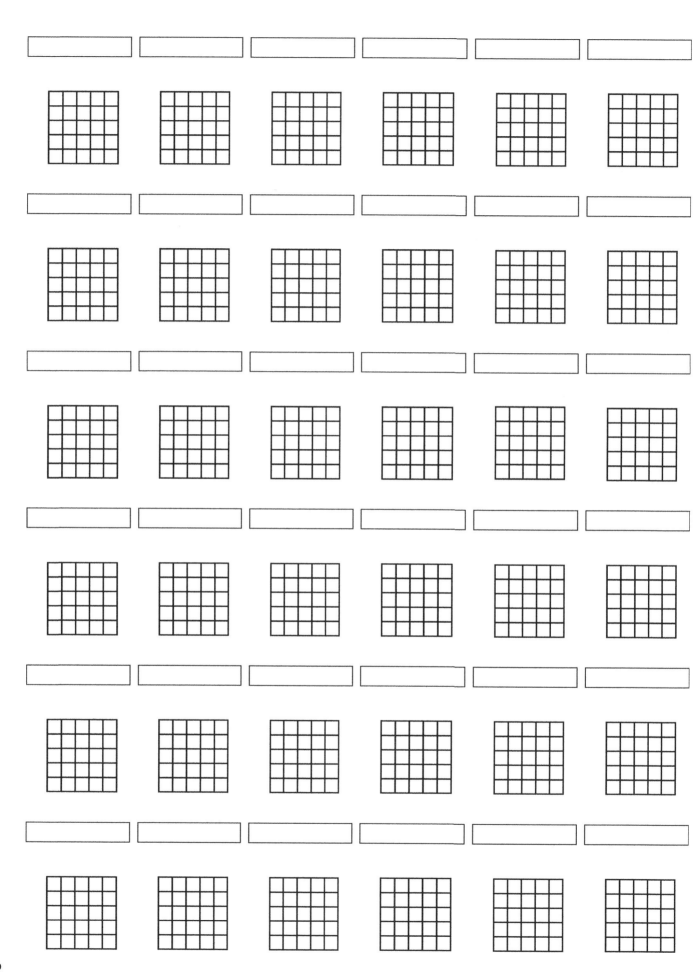

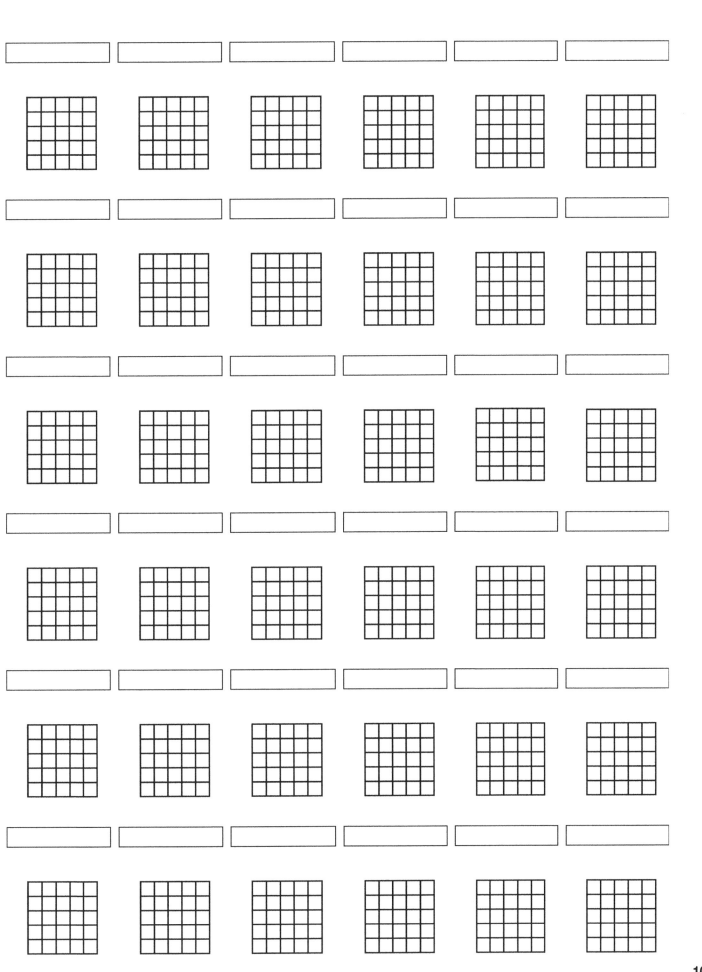

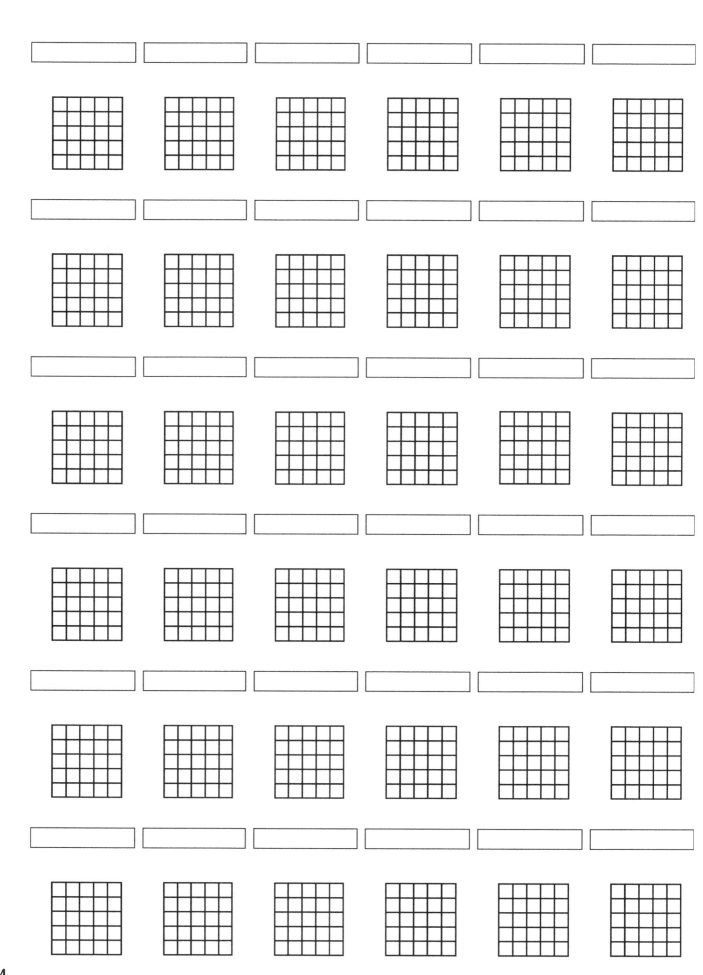

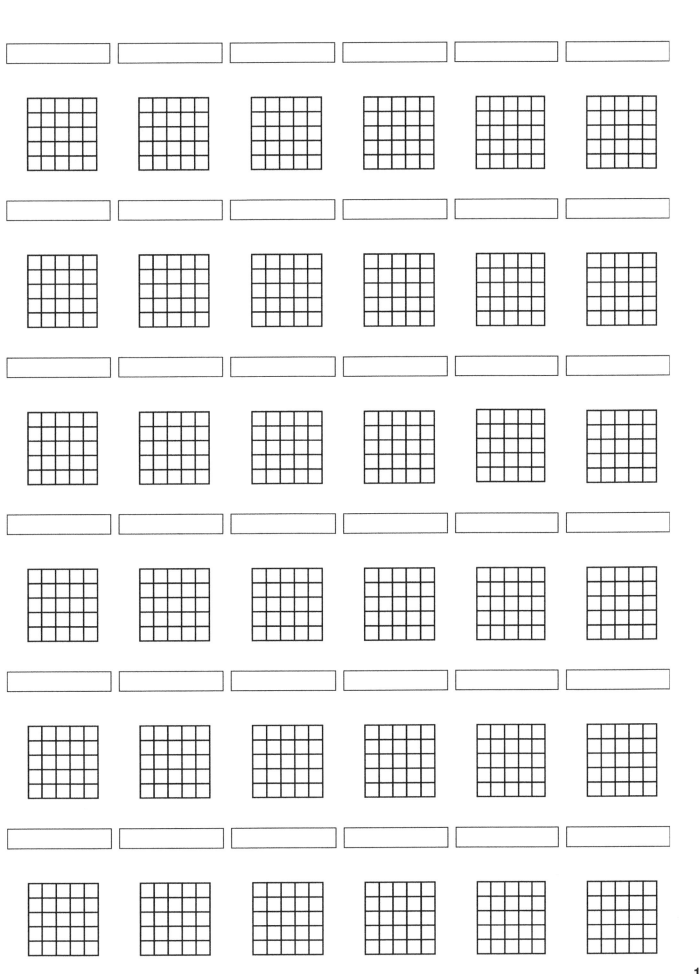

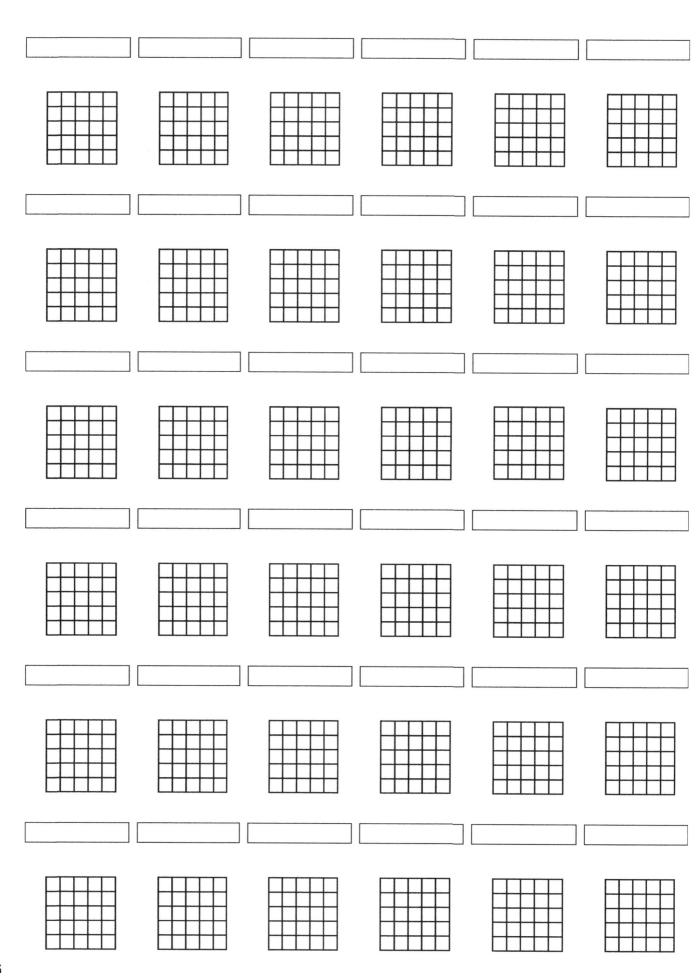

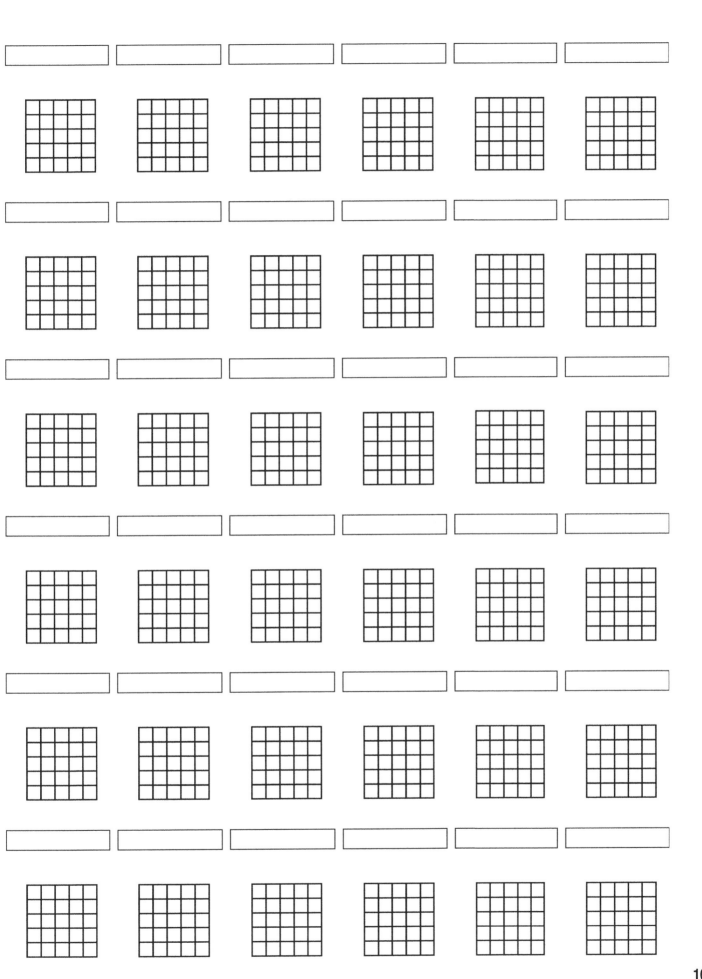

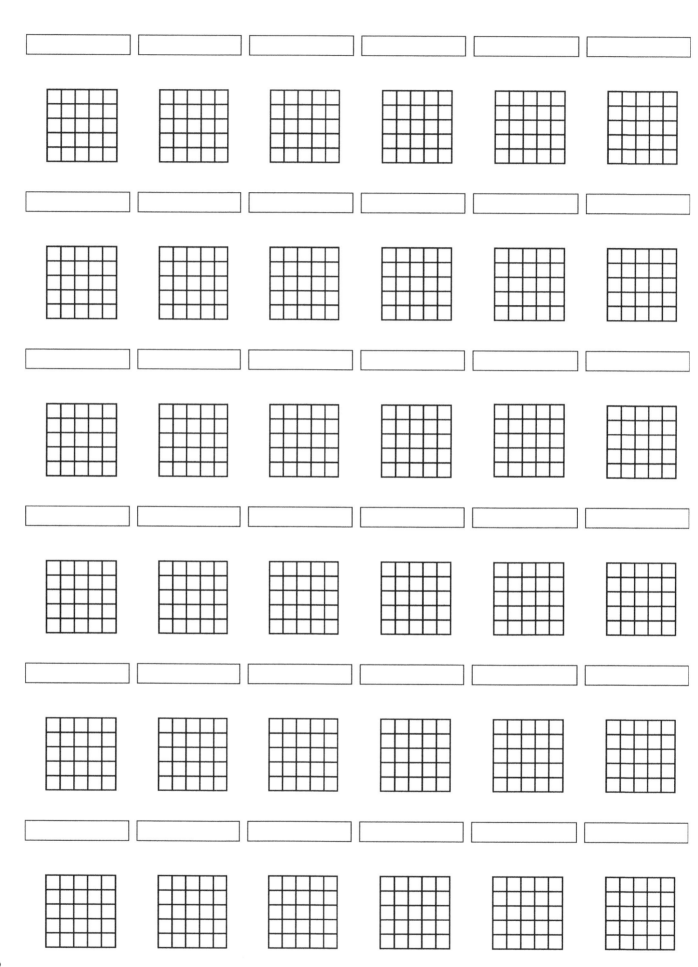

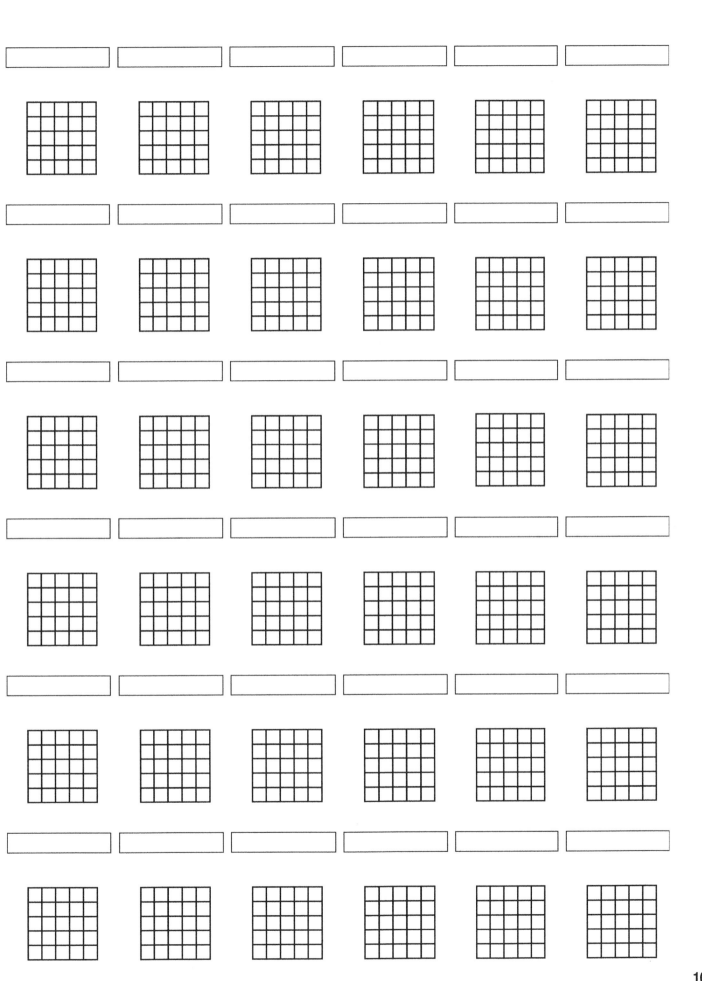

109

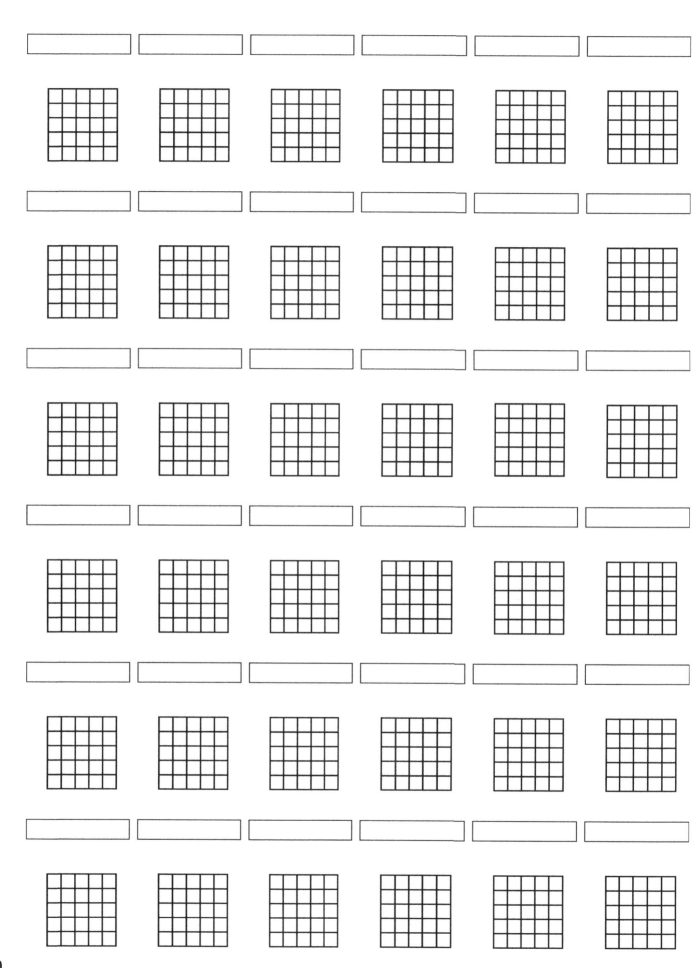

Made in the USA
Las Vegas, NV
23 July 2021